"IMPRISONED"

This book is for everyone.

"IMPRISONED"

Whether incarcerated or not.

"IMPRISONED"

By the web of deceit and lies that Satan has so cleverly woven around the world.

"IMPRISONED"

By SIN to eternal death - if we have not accepted the grace of God through the forgiving power of Jesus Christ.

"IMPRISONED"

Even as professing Christians - if we have allowed things of this world to crowd out the Word of God - if we find ourselves again entrapped by Satan's subtle lies, by the cares and pleasures of this life.

"IMPRISONED"

Until you decide otherwise.

"ESCAPE FROM IMPRISONMENT"

Recommended Dewey Decimal classification: 234
Suggested subject headings: Salvation. Christianity.
Christian Walk.
Library of Congress Catalog Card number: 84-90375

ISBN: 0-932221-17-3

Printed in the United States of America

First Printing 1984
Second Printing 1984
Third Printing 1987
Fourth Printing 1990
Fifth Printing 1992
Sixth Printing 1995

(One hundred and two thousand in print)

Published by "Christians in Action"
Box 571, Columbus, In 47202-0571

ESCAPE FROM IMPRISONMENT

by

CONNELLY L. GRAHAM

Cover Design & Layout
DEBBIE SMALL

Special Edition

Preface

ALL ARE IMPRISONED

CATEGORY # 1.

This book has been written for those who fall into one of three categories. It has been motivated in concern for those of you who actually are behind the bars and walls of our prisons and penal institutions; those who have been charged by the courts and sentenced for breaking some social law as recorded in the law books of our society. It should be of equal interest to those of you who occasionally or repeatedly break many of the same laws of society, but who thus far have escaped being caught or sentenced for your acts or behavior.

CATEGORY # 2.

More specifically however, in a spiritual sense, this book has been written not only for the above group but for *every* MEMBER of the human race. This includes *you* and *me*, whether incarcerated or free, elite or common, young or old, rich or poor, fortunate or unfortunate, churched or unchurched, short or tall, dark or light, or in the majority or minority. Circumstances of location, race, or fortune do not make any difference.

It is written to those who do not yet know the saving power of the Lord Jesus Christ as revealed in the Scriptures and who are as surely bound by the *invisible bars* of Satan to a life of slavery to sin and rebellion to God's established way, as if they were behind the bars of a prison cell. These all shall surely reap, as a result of their continued actions and rejection, the ultimate death row penalty which is *eternal* DEATH.

CATEGORY # 3.

And finally, it is written for those who DO know the Word of God but elect NOT to follow and fully obey its teachings. Each one of us, once again, is given an opportunity to find *forgiveness*, to *change* the direction and course of our lives and to *escape* any penalty involved. This *decision*, as always, is up to you and me as we are individuals with the power of FREE CHOICE.

Connelly L. Graham

GALATIANS 3:22

But the Scripture declares that the whole world is a PRISONER of sin, so that what was promised, being given through faith in Jesus Christ, might be given to those who believe.

Contents

		Page
I.	All Are Imprisoned.	1
II.	Guilty, Judged and Condemned.	9
III.	God's Instruction Manual.	17
IV.	Word of God.	28
V.	Robots Out Of Control	36
VI.	Right Steps to Righteousness	45
VII.	A World of Testing.	72
VIII.	Check Points and Road Signs.	104
IX.	The Present Age of Apostasy.	129
X.	The Future World With Christ.	154
XI.	Wrong Ways Made Right.	167
XII.	Positive Steps to Right Decisions.	189

All Are Imprisoned

DURATION OF THE PENALTY

During this present physical life on earth we may not find ourselves actually behind bars. But we will find ourselves IMPRISONED even though we may be in front of the bars. It may seem an eternity if we are indeed incarcerated, but these man made judgments are still a *temporary*, *temporal* and *transient* condition. On the other hand, God's judgment for each of us will last for an ETERNITY. It will stand forever! So our greater concern, it seems to me, should be with any offense that results in a more drastic and *longer lasting* penalty to us as individuals.

In this life, if we care to observe, we can clearly see the end result, the present plight of a sentenced lawbreaker who has run afoul of the ordinances and laws of our society. The pattern of events is predictable as follows: 1. breaking a law. 2. getting caught and being charged with a crime 3. being convicted and sentenced 4. paying the penalty 5. possible release or future parole.

JUDGMENT DECREED

Most of the time we *fail to see* the cut and dried pattern of events that follow when we transgress God's law. As 'free choice' individuals we are reluctant to recognize even the existence of any such law, let alone to believe that any penalty is attached! We *fail* to *recognize* the severity of our acts and most times we do not even *see* the *connection* between breaking God's law and the sequence of events that might happen to us later on in life. Generally we don't like to consider that the ultimate penalty, which is the SECOND DEATH, already decreed by a just and holy God, will be imposed for all eternity. We just do not want to believe in the *finality* and *severity* of the JUDGMENTS decreed in the Holy Scriptures. Sin however, is revealed in God's Word as "the *transgression* and breaking of God's *Law*" - and DEATH always follows sin. (Ref. I John 3:4)

By analyzing the cause and effect of the penalities involved in breaking social laws (those which we can readily see and experience in our lives and the lives of others around us) we can come to a better understanding as created beings, of our own relationship to God as we try to carry out our own acts of rebellion and self interest in breaking God's established universal and holy ordinances.

RECOGNIZE GOD

To clearly understand our situation we must first of all comprehend *who* we are, *why* we are here, and *where* we are going! It is only as we recognize God as creator of all things, of the Universe, of this earth, of our physical life, and as the sole rewarder of life eternal, will we be able to fathom the destined part we must play as individuals on the *earthly stage*. Until we come to this basic knowledge of truth, life will be nothing more than a *confused state* of existence.

All of us are on center stage, whether knowingly or unknowingly, as we live out this unique *one time* drama on earth called LIFE. It is not a one act play that just came together by chance, as many would like to believe.

It is not a play that will have many happy encores at the end, regardless of how the actors perform. It is *real* life acting in *real* time and all of us here have to step out sooner or later on to center stage.

My desire is that the contents of this book will perhaps provide you the necessary interest, motivation, and above all else the desire to take a second look, to make doubly sure, as you again search out and analyze your reason for existance and the basic truth regarding this all important subject. We will see many road signs, have many options, and hear many voices as we travel life's road. But God's road signs to ETERNAL LIFE are vital, *specific* and *few* in number.

BY CHRIST ALONE

Again I would emphasize each and everyone of us are IMPRISONED, until we break through the shell of self delusion, through the restraints of sin and death which surround us, and reach out for help. Only then can we enter into that glorious new world of life and peace that God provides through Jesus Christ.

This new beginning can *only* be found through the One who has already broken the chains of death and ascended on high to become the Savior of all those who believe and obey. This way is through none other than the LORD JESUS CHRIST, God's son, who was born into this world, who lived and died, for the sins of all mankind. It is He who was without sin yet was crucified and shed his blood for our individual sins. It is He who was resurrected from the grave on the third day and who now sits at the right hand of God the Father awaiting to be our High Priest.

> *The sting of death is sin, and the power of sin is the law. (I Corinthians 15:56)*

But when the time had fully come, God sent his Son, born of a woman, born under law, to redeem those under law, that we might receive the full rights of sons. (Galatians 4:4-5)

IN PRISON

So perhaps *you are actually in prison:* Let's talk about your problems before moving on to other situations. Your incarceration is the end result of a series of acts and actions probably involving many people and perhaps covering a time span of several months or years. It perhaps involved a court, a judge, the law enforcement units, and definitely the victim or victims. Being more specific it included, *yourself.* Much effort, time, and money has in reality been needlessly spent as a result of your unnecessary actions. Many adverse emotions have been created and many lives profoundly affected!

Maybe you are still proclaiming your innocence - rightly or wrongly! Maybe you believe that the penalty you received *far outweighs* the seriousness of the supposed crime committed. Or perhaps, in rare cases, you feel you 'lucked out' and the penalty you received was far less than you actually deserved. Or perhaps, you feel the judgment issued matched the seriousness of the acts you committed against society or the individual.

OUR ATTITUDES

I have tried to simplify and summarize the total range of possible alternative feelings you might have regarding *your* sentence. Of course *none* will be very satisfying! Your feelings on this, to a lesser or greater degree, will be reflected by your *daily* ATTITUDE toward the system and toward the people in the system of which you are now a part. All this in turn will affect your attitude toward others, toward society, and will be reflected, to some extent, in all of the *future thoughts* and ACTIONS of your present life.

OUR THOUGHTS

I doubt if any, who have been physically imprisoned, haven't said or at least thought many times "Why did it have to happen to me?" "Look at all those on the outside who had money to hire a good attorney. They are still running around free"; or "If only I'd been a little more lucky, who'd have ever known?" "Why did fate have to intervene and all those unexpected set of circumstances come together to trip me up?" "Of all the judges in the country and I had to end up being assigned to that one!" "My acts were not half as bad as those others who either beat the rap or got only half the sentence I did." "I was falsely convicted!" "What I did really wasn't all that bad!" "I needed money and had no job." "Society has always put me down." "Now what chance did I have growing up in such a neighborhood and from a broken home." "If you'd been in my situation, you'd be far worse off than I am!"

These and other rational and irrational thoughts have surely crowded through your mind as you have tried to analyze the reasons that led to your present status as a prisoner.

CHRONIC LAWBREAKER

As you look back objectively, with an open mind, perhaps you will find your life has been lived in rebellion to all authority. You have indeed been a *chronic* LAWBREAKER! First, it was getting into trouble with your parents, or the people next door, or with the kids at school or the neighbors down the block. Maybe you were among the *unfortunate* to grow up in a house with no parental control, with a background of family fights and feuds where little or no love was shown. Then came the gang and it's influence on your life. It was probably a thrill at the time to take on the toughie on the block or in the outlying area of the other gang. Or if you were afraid to do that, did you resort to lying, cheating, taking and stealing from aged, innocent or helpless victims? All this for *selfish gain* and to *elevate* the old personal EGO. Then later on you tripped out on alcohol, drugs, amphetamines, barbituates, hallucinogens and pills, until you became an *addicted slave* to all these habits. These of course, lead inevitably to being a slave to more serious crimes against individuals and society to support your new found *enslaving life style.* The pattern is all to familiar and repeats itself with tragic regularity.

Or maybe this was your first experience at having a run-in with the law. All your life you have been thoughtful and careful of the rights of others around you. But in a sudden fit of anger or carelessness, perhaps due to the dreadful effects of drugs, alcohol or selfishness, you committed, on the spur of a moment, a serious crime against another person or persons. Now you find yourself arrested, judged, sentenced and in prison. Maybe for the rest of your natural life.

But the Scripture declares that the whole world is a prisoner of sin, so that what was promised, being given through faith in Jesus Christ, might be given to those who believe.
Before this faith came, we were held prisoners by the law, locked up until faith should be revealed. (Galatians 3:22-23)

It is interesting to note that according to God's standard we are *all* chronic lawbreakers and *all* PRISONERS of sin.

AN UNJUST SENTENCE?

In rare cases perhaps you find yourself completely innocent of the crime with which you've been charged. You were, in essence, in the *wrong place* at the *wrong time* and now find yourself wrongly charged with a crime which you didn't commit; and bitterness, hate, anger welled up inside you against the system that could do such a thing - to commit such a tragic error in taking away your freedom. Perhaps you now lash out at others with cursing; damning and rebuking all things and all people, and resolve in your heart that once you get out and get the chance, you are going to *even up* all the old scores through greater *hatred* and *violence.*

On the other side of the coin, there are many in prison with light sentences, others already paroled, who according to the seriousness of their crimes against society and individuals, should still be incarcerated. Perhaps there are some who in a few months or years have obtained a parole, and immediately started a life of crime all over again, with one apprehension after another, only to beat the rap again, and *again*, and AGAIN, until it has become a normal way of life. This has cost the state and society hundreds of thousands of dollars to process these cases through the legal system in the name of so called human rights. More importantly, the lives of dozens of innocent and honest victims have been wrecked and destroyed.

What does society really owe those who have never known anything since early childhood but wanton DESTRUCTION? Does it owe more *freedom* to do more of the same at the expense of the upright innocent?

WHERE IS JUSTICE?

Maybe you've seen on television some of the fat cats in government or business organizations whom you feel are getting away with crimes far worse than you ever committed - the so called *white-collared* crimes of money, of influence and payoffs. Your anger and hatred simmers while they are still running around *free*, still gathering in money under every pretense for their every whim. Many are even re-elected to office with great public acclaim - while their deeds are seemingly *forgotten*. You and I cry out *"where is justice?"* Is there no justice anywhere?" "Why are they not apprehended, judged and sentenced as I was?" You ask, "Are they not just as deserving of punishment as I am?" And on this score you are *undoubtedly right*!

Why have I taken the time to scrounge around and pull some of these old feelings and skeletons out of the closet; feelings that maybe you've spent months trying to put behind you and forget! First of all, it is to get you to identify with me as I try to make the next two points, which I'll just note briefly now, with more detail later.

Guilty, Judged and Condemned

SATAN IS IN CONTROL

The point is this, even if you've been misled in hoping for something different - "THE WORLD WE LIVE IN IS FULL OF EVIL AND INJUSTICE - from top to bottom!" Sorry, but its the only world we have at the present time.

> ***So justice is driven back, and righteousness stands at a distance; truth has stumbled in the streets, honesty cannot enter.***
> ***Truth is nowhere to be found, and whoever shuns evil becomes a prey.***
> ***The Lord looked and was displeased that there was no justice. (Isaiah 59:14-15)***

For the most part *all* of the world systems are run and influenced by evil and sinful men who obtain advantage by money, intrigue, payoffs and deceit. This is not a pretty picture but this is the true nature of man as he is influenced by Satan. This is because *Satan* is now in total CONTROL! "He is," the scriptures say, "the prince of the power of the air of this world." The present world systems are his to influence and try to control.

> ***As for you, you were dead in your transgressions and sins, in which you used to live when you followed the ways of this world and of the ruler of the kingdom of the air, the spirit who is now at work in those who are disobedient. (Ephesians 2:1-2).***

Since the fall of man in the garden of Eden, when man rejected God's way as recorded in Genesis 3, God has allowed Satan, through help of unregenerate man to *try* to *rule* this earth *without* GOD. What you see around you and in you, is *Satan's Way* and man's selfish will coming to fruition. It is *not* a result of environment and circumstance. It is the *end* RESULT of rejecting God's way which will bring peace, joy and happiness, if followed.

As we analyze our actions we find ourselves a victim of Satan's lies and influence in more ways than we first imagined. Besides God's will and Satan's self will there are now three or four billion independent wills, most opposed to God, some opposed to Satan, but the majority opposed to each other. Satan longs to capture all of these adverse wills in worship to himself but only succeeds in stirring up the stew.

The second point we should note is this. If we are indeed still being led by Satan, then we are surely on a *one way* trip that can only lead to imprisonment, loneliness, and eventually the second death, which is *eternal* separation from God!

> ***But the cowardly, the unbelieving, the vile, the murderers, the sexually immoral, those who practice magic arts, the idolater and the liars — their place will be in the fiery lake of burning sulfur. This is the second death."***
> ***(Revelation 21:8)***
>
> ***By the same word the present heavens and earth are reserved for fire, being kept for the day of judgement and destruction of ungodly men.***
> ***(II Peter 3:7)***

There will be no unexpected rainbow, freedom, or bright lights found around any corner in our immediate or long range future if we do not make a change.

TAKE A TRIP

Any trip taken on any road, whether by chance or by a detailed study of a map, will eventually reach some destination. It's basic, but all trips have a beginning and an ending connected by a mid-course travel. I remember a few years ago when in high school my friends and I used to play a little game on a Sunday afternoon out in the countryside of Indiana with a borrowed Model A Ford. We would start driving and at every mile cross road intersection of the rock covered country roads we would flip a coin to see if we should turn right, turn left, or go straight ahead. Believe me, we ended up before many miles in some very interesting places which we usually had never seen before. Sometimes the journey would end in a farmer's barnyard, or facing into an impassable stream without a bridge, or down a dead end lane.

Regardless of how we travel on any trip, when we get far enough down the road we've taken, we can always look back and ascertain how the early twists and turns actually dictated the course we are being forced to take on the last part of our journey.

MID-COURSE CORRECTION

The same holds true with your life and mine! This is one reason that I took us on an excursion earlier of some past reflections and thoughts. Certain basic decisions, influences and actions, made during the early or mid-course of a life can surely dictate within limits, our *final* or *ultimate end.* Unless, a new course of direction is *desired* and put into ACTION! As with all missile flights a mid-course correction should always be considered and used in order to reach a final DESIRED DESTINATION.

Cause and effect always goes hand in hand - whether they be separated by *miles* or by *years*. We will surely and inevitably *reap* what we have *sown* earlier! Payday will always arrive, as perhaps to our dismay, we have already found out to some degree. God says, over and over that the pay or "the *wages* of sin is *death*" - the *second* DEATH! (Ref. Romans 6:23). One part of the prior paragraph is of such importance I'd like to repeat it so we don't miss it. *A course correction*, a *new road*, can be selected at anytime, while you are still alive and willing to MAKE A CHANGE!

Re-read the last sentence again and again to memorize it as it is very important to your ultimate welfare and destination. Mid-course corrections are not only desirable but *essential* in order to arrive at a predetermined goal, whether for a missile flight or for a life. Time, present circumstances or age, have no bearing on our willingness to choose and to put into operation a course correction.

YOU ARE HERE

All of us have seen those diagrams and maps put up in large shopping centers or big malls with a big red arrow painted on them that say "YOU ARE HERE." Under the arrow is found a diagram of the facility showing all the corridors, stores, aisles, doors and exits. You may have wandered in aimlessly to find yourself at your present location. But you may be lost as to known direction or destination. Whenever you look inquiringly at the arrow that says "YOU ARE HERE", you can put aside all the twists and turns and wrong choices you previously may have made to arrive at your present location. You can be assured of only one thing - '*Your Present Position.*'

You now have a clear cut choice. You can try to find your way out by the way you came in, which under some circumstances might be pretty hopeless, or you can put aside all your past wanderings, all that you've done in the past; plant your feet firmly down in front of the big red arrow that says "you are here," and accept that simple but revealing fact. Then without all the influence of *emotions* and *actions* of the past which put you in your present spot, look up at the map and study it for the quickest and most positive way out of your situation.

This can be a good example of our life and how we can correct bad choices. Today you are in *real time* standing in front of the big red arrow that says "Stop - you are here." *This is your position;* not on a side trip to a shopping center, but in a real one time life situation. And if we are honest about the revealed facts, it may not seem to be too great a location. For God says: 'ALL have sinned and come short of the glory of God' (Ref. Romans 3:23) - ALL are deserving of death. So all of us have to crowd toe to toe in front of the big red arrow that says "you are here" as we are judged equally guilty of transgression of God's laws.

> ***All have turned away, they have together become worthless; there is no one who does good, not even one." (Romans 3:12)***

Before the change, in God's sight there are *none worse* or *none better* than others, nor none more worthy than others! There are none closer or farther behind! God has provided the same "*way* of *escape*" for all of us. There are no alternate routes or byways. The only way has been outlined in detail. Some of you will be concerned. You will respond to God's way and find safety and life. Others will sink back into the oblivion of darkness and death because you do not believe the sign and the warning that God's map provides.

> ***We must pay more careful attention, therefore, to what we have heard, so that we do not drift away. For if the message spoken by angels was binding, and every violation and disobedience received its just punishment, how shall we escape if we ignore such a great salvation? This salvation, which was first announced by the Lord, was confirmed to us by those who heard him. (Hebrews 2:1-3)***

Still others of you will believe you are exempt for one reason or another! *This choice*, this option, this way, is what this book is all about. It is to proclaim there is a *better way* - an *only WAY* - and that is GOD'S WAY, (not man's).

> ***Blessed is the man who does not walk in the counsel of the wicked or stand in the way of sinners or sit in the seat of mockers. But his delight is in the law of the Lord, and on his law he meditates day and night. (Psalms 1: 1-2)***

There is only one road map, one book which shows that way and that is the HOLY BIBLE. Man made books, such as this one, are only useful as a reference if they direct and point you to that one source of information and truth.

ALL IN THE SAME BOAT

We read in God's word that He is no respector of persons.

> ***Then Peter began to speak: "I now realize how true it is that God does not show favoritism but***

accepts men from every nation who fear him and do what is right. (Acts 10: 34-35)

We may find ourselves in different circumstances from others, as different as day is from night, but our present condition, status, or circumstances will have no bearing on God's penalty decree, because it applies to ALL men EVERYWHERE. We have *all* transgressed or broken God's Holy Laws. The "*all*" includes all races, both sexes, young, old, rich, poor, educated, illiterate, free, incarcerated, churched, unchurched, known, unknown, leaders or followers-everyone that has ever been born on earth, except Jesus Christ.

On a personal basis you and I, as individuals, are *no exception* to this decree of God.

> ***"If we claim we have not sinned, we make him out to be a liar and his word has no place in our lives. (I John 1:10)***

OUR UNWORTHINESS

God talks much about carnal man's unworthiness - his self righteousness as compared to the RIGHTEOUSNESS that He can accept.

> ***All of us have become like one who is unclean, and all our righteous acts are like filthy rags; we all shrivel up like a leaf, and like the wind our sins sweep us away. No one calls on your name or strives to lay hold of you; for you have hidden your face from us and made us waste away because of our sins. (Isaiah 64: 6-7)***

I'm sure you will point out there are tens of thousands,

perhaps millions of honest decent, sincere people in the world, like yourself perhaps, who show a lot of love, kindness and concern for others, who have never made a decision for Christ. What about them? Don't their pious efforts earn them a few brownie awards? This degree of good which is very applaudable by the world and readily accepted by self is *not good enough* for a Holy God. We

have all been CHRONIC LAW-BREAKERS in God's sight! The best of man-made righteousness according to God is as filthy rags in His sight. This is hard to swallow, but it's true! Many people, especially *those* afflicted with disease of *self righteousness* cannot accept that this statement applies to them.

God says, "the human heart is desperately *wicked* - who can know it"? Surely not man! And all this time we thought we were something great and perhaps quite acceptable because we have NOT yet *fully comprehended* by our finite minds, the RIGHTEOUSNESS and HOLINESS and MAJESTY of God, our Creator. We have tried to sell our version of righteousness and mix it in with God's *holy righteousness* hoping somehow to get it accepted by our concept of a gullible God. Breaking of the man-made laws of society is but a reflection of the ailing condition of the human heart in its effort to rebel and to break God's perfect law. If we can't meet God's standard of righteousness we try to set up our own comfortable standards to live by. If these don't work then we shift down into a lower gear until we become comfortable with what self-righteousness and conscience we have. In fact, even the highest standard which we could select by our own logic and reasoning is totally unacceptable to God.

God's Instruction Manual

GOD'S LAW GIVEN

Most of the social laws on the law books are actually based in part on the moral code of God given on Mt. Sinai to the nation of Israel some 1500 years before the birth of Christ. In the 6th chapter of Exodus there is given a detailed account of God first thundering out His moral laws to the human race by His writing of the Ten Commandments on tablets of stone for Moses and the chosen people of Israel. God there and then chose a people through which he could deal with on earth and so He gave them His decree, His laws, and ordinances for individual and social behavior.

But when the children of Israel saw the thunder and lightning, the earthquake and smoke, and heard God's voice they were terrified and had no desire to face such an *awesome* God. They cried unto Moses as they experienced God's presence even afar off. They pleaded for Moses to *go* talk to God. They promised faithfully under such conditions "His laws we will keep! These we will do." All this until the sights and sounds diminished and then they were soon back to their old habits of sin and unrighteousness.

GOD'S RIGHTEOUSNESS

God's holiness is so HOLY, His *righteousness* is so far above our comprehension of righteousness and His *way* is so far above man's ways, that our finite minds cannot really comprehend His glory and righteousness. His MAJESTY is so great that all who have ever experienced the presence of even one of His Holy angels (His messengers) have fallen prostrate on the ground with no breath of life left in them until given strength and lifted up supernaturally. The pot cannot compare to or comprehend the mind of the potter that created and shaped it, and we, the created being, although of the highest of intellect, cannot fully comprehend the thoughts and the grandeur of the *creator* that designed and created us. Man's limited and finite intellectual capacity and his comparison to only experiences and knowledge obtained in this physical life, restricts his ability as he tries to comprehend the truths regarding God's description of Himself and His attributes.

> ***The heavens declare the glory of God; the skies proclaim the work of his hands. Day after day they pour forth speech; night after night they display knowledge. There is no speech or language where their voice is not heard. Their voice goes out into all the earth, their words to the ends of the world. In the heavens he has pitched a tent for the sun. (Psalms 19:1-4)***

MT. SINAI

My wife and I have climbed Mt. Sinai in the southern Arabian peninsula where this law was communicated to Moses. A more desolate, isolated, hot spot, I have never experienced. A more rugged and tiring mountainous climb I can't remember, although I've hunted deer and elk in the mountains of Colorado for years. To my amazement some of the rocks on top of Sinai are still covered by a thick black coating about one sixteenth of an inch thick in spots; much of which has fallen off in splotches. In other places it can be scratched off with a knife. Something has literally burned and charred the top of the mountain and the rocks are split in great fissures by past earthquakes. What more physical evidence do we need to affirm that it was indeed engulfed in fire and brimstone as noted by God in verses 16-19 of Exodus, Chapter 19? Every aspect of the Mt. Sinai area, including the one and only flat valley about 10-20 miles long, right below Mt. Sinai where the camels now roam freely, was a revelation of truth. There the loose rocks that normally covered the valley floor were stacked against the surrounding mountains as if they were carried out by someone to make a smooth camp site on this vast empty, desolate valley floor. The Israelites undoubtedly were the ones as they camped in this very spot for the year they were at Sinai receiving God's instructions as a people. This and other evidence testifies to the accuracy of the Scriptures as the word of God is revealed on every hand in historical and anthropological discoveries.

THE TEN COMMANDMENTS

I feel it necessary to repeat the law of God, given on Sinai to Moses and the Israelites. They are the *one true* STANDARD of all standards and should be the BASIS OF ALL laws, codes and ordinances of mankind today. Found in Exodus 20:1-17 they are summarized as follows:

I. You shall have no other Gods besides Me.

II. You shall not worship any graven image.

III. You shall not take the Name of the Lord thy God in vain.

IV. Remember the Sabbath Day to keep it holy.

V. Honor your Father and your Mother.

VI. You shall not murder.

VII. You shall not commit adultery.

VIII. You shall not steal.

IX. You shall not bear false witness.

X. You shall not covet anything that is your neighbor's.

Believe it or not, God did not give these laws *as a means by which* man could SAVE himself. But sin brought to light by this very law CONDEMNS man and shows his dire *need* of a savior. God fore-knew that man was *incapable* of keeping all these basic universal commandments.

But sin, seizing the opportunity afforded by the commandment, produced in me every kind of covetous desire. For apart from law, sin is dead. Once I was alive apart from law; but when the commandment came, sin sprang to life and I died. I found that the very commandment that was intended to bring life actually brought death. For sin, seizing the opportunity afforded by the commandment, deceived me, and through the commandment put me to death.

(Romans 7:8-11)

God says if we have broken one, we are a law breaker and in essence have broken all of them. Prior to the age of law and until the law was given, man did not know sin and sin was not accounted to him. God's decree or punishment for those who do sin is DEATH; first, the physical death then later the second death! The physical death decree however was imposed on Adam and Eve and all members of the human race for rebellion even before the law was given. This is not a 6-month or 12 year imprisonment or a slap on the wrist and probation, but DEATH (the ultimate death row penalty). Appeals are useless after that judgment and sentence is carried out.

> ***Therefore, just as sin entered the world through one man, and death through sin, and in this way death came to all men, because all sinned — for before the law was given, sin was in the world. But sin is not taken into account when there is no law. (Romans 5:12-13)***

Our man-made social laws are for the most part a reflection of these basic laws. This is known as the Judeo-Christian ethic. Of course, man because of necessity, has broken down each law into hundreds and thousands of individual laws and ordinances and codes for every state, municipality and county, in an attempt to cover every aspect of the *interfaces* of human existence! These are broken down to try and define even the speed at which we can drive a car in each specific area. Think how many laws and ordinances are imposed upon us in just driving across a city with its hundreds of different speed zones, traffic lights, and parking regulations. If we break any of these codes we can incur a fine, a reprimand, or a lockup - depending on the seriousness of the offense. These all attempt to regulate our actions and proper relationships required in a crowded society. Most man-made laws are well intentioned at first. Some are good when first passed, but later can become obsolete. Most laws are quite necessary for an orderly society. Of course all could be eliminated if indeed we all kept the one law of "love for our neighbor."

Now God *did not* set up His standards or moral laws to restrict our movements or cause us unnecessary problems, to harm us, or to take away from our joy or happiness. On the contrary, they are given because a *wise* and *knowing* God knows His creation well enough to know that harmony, peace, and happiness can NEVER EXIST in the universe as long as the rebellion that is found in the human heart is given free reign for expression. God's law reveals and identifies that rebellion! And so a weeding out process begins.

GOD KNOWS BEST

There can be no place in the midst of the holiness and righteousness of God's abode for SIN. Sin would be out of place in such an environment like the proverbial wild bull with 6-foot horns in the finest crowded china shop with 3-foot aisles. Likewise there will be no chance for peace, harmony, or happiness on earth until the perfect law of God is placed in *each* human heart.

> ***But the wisdom that comes from heaven is first of all pure; then peace loving, considerate, submissive, full of mercy and good fruit, impartial and sincere. Peacemakers who sow in peace raise a harvest of righteousness.***
> ***(James 3:17-18)***

Only that which makes an inner change in the human heart can redirect a wayward soul. Man written codes and ordinances are in a sense like locking the barn door after the horse has wandered outside. They don't keep us from breaking the law. They just impose loss or penalty when we get caught. God gave His moral law to *convict man;* later poured out His grace and love through Jesus Christ so that His creation could be *accounted* worthy to receive it, and then to keep it, in a spiritual sense. God wants us to have REAL LIFE and enjoy unprecedented joy and happiness, not the *dregs* that

Satan has dished up for our lust and entertainment. It is just this simple! God as creator knows what WILL WORK and what will cause us, His creation, *harm and destruction.* He knows what will *build up* and not tear down, what will bring ETERNAL LIFE and not eternal death.

Many times we do not believe these words of wisdom from God but have to choose that which seems so logical to our own deceitful human hearts. Our way, of course, is not always in accordance with God's *will* thus problems and troubles soon arise. Far too often we set *self* and *self interests* above all else as our guiding light. This is just the opposite of love - the love of God and the love for our neighbor as ourselves, which is the great and foremost commandment of God. Love is OUTFLOWING concern for others - the other is possessive gain for self edification. One is the way to 'get', the other way is to 'give'.

Many have not realized that the *love of self* (defiance of God's way for our own self-way) is the *basic* SIN of man. We have set ourselves up in self dependency, in defiance of God's way, trying to *usurp* His power and authority over our lives. But God says, "There is a way which seemeth right unto man but the end thereof is the way of death." (Ref. Proverbs 14:12). How true! A good way to remember the right definition of sin is recollect that it is the selfish personal pronoun 'I' found in the middle of S(I)N that makes it what it is.

SINS - EVIDENCE OF A SINNER

Yes, hate, gossip, murder, adultery, cheating, lying and stealing are just the everyday evidence of the basic sin of man hidden in the selfish human heart.

To the pure, all things are pure, but to those who

are corrupted and do not believe, nothing is pure. In fact, both their minds and consciences are corrupted. (Titus 1:15)

SELF DEPENDENCY
IS
"SIN"
IS
DISOBEDIENCE
TO GODS WAY...

Since death is the payment of sin, all shall experience the death of the body, if we are not translated; but we don't have to experience the *second death,* except by choice.

As we look around this old terra firma and see the order and harmony of all creation and note specifically the confusion, tensions, pressures and actions of our fellow travelers, it surely doesn't take an analyst or a college professor to realize that something is really wrong with this world - and *with man.* Man has given a multitude of reasons for his actions but God has given only one - SIN!

It is the way of man that follows SELF and not God's way that is leading to sorrows, confusion, wars, chaos, and the destruction we see. Do you still think the world will get better and better as time goes on? GOD DOESN'T. He says, "Evil men and seducers shall wax worse and worse, deceiving and being deceived." (Ref. II Timothy 3:13). And this we can now clearly see if we but objectively look at what has happened and is taking place around us.

As Jesus was sitting on the Mount of Olives, the disciples came to him privately. "Tell us," they said, "when will this happen, and what will be the sign of your coming and of the end of the age?"

Jesus answered: "Watch out that no one deceives you. For many will come in my name, claiming, 'I am the Christ,' and will deceive many. You will hear of wars and rumors of wars, but see to it that you are not alarmed. Such things must happen, but the end is still to come.

Nation will rise against nation, and kingdom against kingdom. There will be famines and earthquakes in various places. All these are the beginning of birth pains.

"Then you will be handed over to be persecuted and put to death, and you will be hated by all nations because of me. At that time many will turn away from the faith and will betray and hate each other, and many false prophets will appear and deceive many people. Because of the increase of wickedness, the love of most will grow cold, but he who stands firm to the end will be saved. (Matthew 24:3-13)

We are a special creation of God! We are made in the *image* of God and as such are given the power of free choice and decision.

Then God said, "Let us make man in our image, in our likeness, and let them rule over the fish of the sea and the birds of the air, over the livestock, over all the earth, and over all the creatures that move along the ground."

So God created man in his own image, in the image of God he created him; male and female he created them. (Genesis 1:26-27)

But what a mess we have made by our choices and decisions that have been based on our own human logic. However God has not left us on our own to find basic truths by trial and error. He has provided us with guide lines, a rule book, an instruction manual - the HOLY SCRIPTURES. In it He has outlined very carefully the *only* way to eternal life and the *only* way to good health, long life and happiness on earth. He has also described in detail the way which will lead us to trouble and to *tragedy;* the way which is known scripturally as "the way of the world!" In a real sense the Bible is God's *instruction and operating* MANUAL for His greatest creation, Man.

OWNERS MANUAL

God gave us His new creation, this instruction manual, The Holy Bible to identify sin and to guide us in right decisions and instructions. We should read, consider and follow the Holy Scriptures as faithfully as we use manufacturer's manuals for the physical items we buy.

> ***All Scripture is God-breathed and is useful for teaching, rebuking, correcting and training in righteousness, so that the man of God may be thoroughly equipped for every good work.***
> ***(II Timothy 3:16-17)***

In a lesser degree don't we as humans, when we design or create a new mechanical or electronic product and issue instructions for its proper use, follow God's example here on earth? When I buy something of value there is always included an instruction sheet or manual of DO'S and DON'TS for its operation. In fact, I have a whole file drawer full of such books which I have filed away over the years from past purchases. Why are manuals issued? To arbitrarily and maliciously restrict the use of the object? *Of course not!* They are issued so the owner can enjoy the *longest* and *best use* of the product, whether it be a TV set, a computer, a dryer or washer, a car or tractor, or an air conditioner.

If we fail to change the oil in the car engine or at least keep it at its proper level, dire circumstances have been predicted in the owner's manual - it will eventually *destruct.*

We can ignore the manual or not believe it, and pour in water instead of oil and the engine will follow the same predicted course and DESTRUCT. The creator and designer knows best, whether he be human for material items or God for His creation. So we go ahead and plug a 110 volt air conditioner into a 220 volt AC circuit and the smoke pours out, as predicted, before final destruction. It then is of no further value to us or others. All this will happen each time regardless of whether we believe the owner's manual or not.

DESIGNER AND CREATOR

We are the designer and creator for these mechanical and electrical products. We have *foreknowledge* of what *will* and *will not* work, what will protect, and what will destroy. We as designers are laying down the standards, the rules, circumstances, or laws under which the units are designed to operate and give the greatest usage and the *longest life.* Doesn't God as creator have the same *knowledge, option* and *prerogatives* for us as created beings of His? Can't we at least concede the logic of this? Do you have any doubt that God, as creator of the Universe, the earth and all of life, knows what WILL or WILL NOT work in the human cycle of life. He designed us a physical being, made in His image, with a capacity to choose and capable of receiving *spiritual* LIFE. He knows better than we what will kill and maim; what will bring good health and happiness and joy - and has warned what will bring sorrow, shame, illness, and destruction. What foolishness for the thing created *to try* and take control. The basic issue is whether WE BELIEVE the manual or not - not in the accuracy of the manual. But the very nature of Satan raises the question, "Yeah, hath God said . . .?" (Ref. Genesis 3:1). And lost man parrots - "I don't believe in His word. In fact, *I don't even believe in a God* - I am supreme in myself!"

Word of God

Do you or do you not believe in the Word of God? Have you placed your faith and trust in the promises of God's Word? I trust that you have. If so, may these few pages renew and increase your faith in the Son of God.

> ***I write these things to you who believe in the name of the Son of God so that you may know that you have eternal life. This is the assurance we have in approaching God: that if we ask anything according to his will, he hears us.***
> ***(I John 5:13-14)***

If you do not *now* believe, then these next few pages can be worth more to you than any possession you've ever acquired on earth. God says, 'What shall it profit a man if he gain the whole world and lose his own soul?' (Ref. Mark 8: 36). Good question! I would not even have room in this book to make an outline of the many steps whereby you can prove that the Scriptures are the Word of God. Contrary to popular opinion of the masses and those who would destroy the Christian faith, the Word of God *can be proven.*

The Bible speaks with known authority on eternal life. It describes it's existence, its composition, and most importantly, the pathway that must be followed to its eternal shores. And you can prove without a doubt that the Bible is the Holy Word of God, that it is the citadel of wisdom, of truth, and understanding. The Bible is the revelation of God's Will to man and is not a collection of myth and fable of ancient history, as some would have us believe.

Perhaps you have said, "It's hard for me to believe the Bible is the inspired Word of God." Answer one question then: Have you studied it completely enough to prove your question without doubt? For example, have you read it through from cover to cover in an attitude of seeking and learning? Have you proven to yourself beyond a shadow of a doubt that its hundreds of prophecies have not and are not coming into fulfillment? Can you absolutely prove that God is NOT the Creator of the Universe, of which you are a part, even though the Bible declares He is? Do you have positive proof to the contrary? Do you have undeniable proof that the detailed Biblical records of events and of the people of the past are false? Or have you taken someone else's ideas and words and adopted them? The past 6000 years of recorded human history and anthropological discoveries prove otherwise! You must weigh fiction and fantasy with FACT.

> ***I want you to know, brothers, that the gospel I preached is not something that man made up. I did not receive it from any man, nor was I taught it; rather, I received it by revelation from Jesus Christ. (Galations 1:11-12)***

PROOF OF THE BIBLE

By the way, there are six ways by which you can test the Bible for its truth. And these ways are not applicable to *any other* book that man has in his possession:

1. Harmony and ORDER of the Scriptures.
2. SCIENTIFIC verity of the Word.
3. RELIABILITY of prophecy.
4. The PROGRESSIVE UNFOLDING of events and ages.
5. The POWER of the Word.
6. RECORDS of secular history.

God says as noted previously, "The wages of sin is death". He then outlines the results of such sin, even as it affects our lives here on earth. And so we note that the first *death* is the lot of *every man.* Would you care to dispute the first part of this statement regarding physical death or argue that death is not the lot of man? Do you believe that death is really just happenstance, that it is just an unfortunate development in the scheme of things. Scripture gives the only plausible reason for the fact of *death,* or for life.

For centuries man has sought for the long lost Fountain of Youth. He has tried desperately to prolong his present life using various means. By the use of antibiotics, drugs, pills and modern surgical methods, he has been able to extend his life span here in the United States to an average of 70 plus years. Thousands of years ago the Bible foretold the present age of man: "The days of our years are three score and ten." (Ref. Psalms 90:10). 70 YEARS! Rather close comparison, don't you think?

Space travel is measured by time, not distance. Our life is measured the same way. And time is running out on each individual in this world from the moment they are born. Each person must face the very same issue regardless of position, age, wealth, or location. This inexorable *issue* of our present life is Death. "Wherefore, as by one man (Adam) sin entered into the world; and death by sin; and so death passed upon all men, for that all have sinned." (Ref. Romans 5:12).

HOPE OF LIFE AFTER DEATH

There is nothing that man himself can do to stave off this death decree. In addition to the pioneering spirit inherent in every individual is the hope of ETERNAL LIFE, a life beyond this sentence of death. This dream

has been generated within every individual who has ever trod upon the shores of earth. For the millions, it has remained only a dream, an illusion, a passing thought. Many have been reluctant to think about it because preceding it is 'death' which is a 'No-No.' Thus very little serious thinking is spent on this most important subject!

Why have so many, so flippantly, so carelessly, cast aside this dream without trying to verify truth of such an important and far reaching HOPE? Even if it were only a rumor, heard from some distant world, isn't the goal so *great*, the effects so *stupendous*, the prize so *fabulous*, that it should demand our immediate attention? Couldn't we better spend our time, the days, weeks, months, even years of a lifetime in verifying the truth of its existence; and more importantly once assured that it does exist, to find the pathway that leads to its golden shores? Wouldn't it be worth your while to spend the next few days, months, or even years of your existence to discover and acquire these truths?

Men have given their lives in vain attempts to find the fountain of youth. What could conceivably be more important to you in this life with death awaiting just ahead, than to find the way to obtain ETERNAL LIFE after death.

> ***On one occasion an expert in the law stood up to test Jesus. "Teacher," he asked, "What must I do to inherit eternal life?"***
>
> ***What is written in the Law?" he replied. "How do you read it?"***
>
> ***He answered: " 'Love the Lord your God with all your heart and with all your soul and with all your strength and with all your mind'; and, 'Love***

your neighbor as yourself.' "

"You have answered correctly," Jesus replied. "Do this and you will live." (Luke 10:25-28)

How much time have you spent on verification of this all important goal, ETERNAL LIFE, before reaching your decision to ignore all hope of obtaining it? Or do you think it will be automatic? How can you prove an allegedly good fishing stream without fishing, or a good recipe without tasting? How can you be in a position to properly reject or accept this goal without thorough study and analysis of the facts? Some things we don't have to concern ourselves with and they will take place regardless of our knowing or caring - such as the sunrise tomorrow, the storm clouds, the seasons, aging or death. But this is not the case with eternal life. It is only obtained by a will of the mind; by our initiative and action.

This same God who has given us our present existence, who established all the laws by which the universe operates, who established the galaxies and hung them out across the voids of space, has also declared in the Holy Scriptures ... "The gift of God is ETERNAL LIFE through Jesus Christ our Lord." (Ref. Romans 6:23)

How can we, as individuals, obtain this gift so graciously and freely promised? Is it perhaps by our good works, good intentions, or our man-made and man-observed sacrifices? Can it be obtained by occasionally abstaining from a few lusts and desires of the flesh? Or, do we wishfully think that maybe this life will all fade away as a bad dream and we will wake up some bright morning in an eternal home on some distant shore without any decision or effort on our part? No, the same God who has created all things, has also declared and promised this eternal existence, *not to all*, but only to those who OBEY His commands.

If you obey my commands, you will remain in my love, just as I have obeyed my Father's commands and remain in his love. (John 15:10)
The world and its desires pass away, but the man who does the will of God lives forever. (I John 2:17)

Even by human reasoning we must admit that only the Creator of the universe and of this life would have the power to establish and give eternal life. It is obvious that we, as human beings, do not have it within our power to do this. And since the Creator has declared its existence, doesn't it stand to reason that He and He alone has the authority to set the rules for obtaining it? Or would we, in our human pride and foolishness, try to usurp all such right from Him and try to establish our own rules, now that He has created eternal life and declared it?

I wonder which has it been in your case? ... your wishful thinking, or God's established way?

"Why do the nations rage and the peoples plot in vain? The kings of the earth take their stand and the rulers gather together against the Lord and against his Anointed One. "Let us break their chains," they say, "and throw off their fetters." The One enthroned in heaven laughs; the Lord scoffs at them. (Psalms 2:1-4)

A POOR BET

Maybe you're still a skeptic and words do not mean a thing since your mind is already made up. Let me present you with real, cold, earthly logic. Forget for the moment all we know about the universe around us and God's revelation of Himself. Maybe you are still thinking that God doesn't exist and that the millions and millions of intelligent Christians of all walks of life that have lived in the last 2,000 years were deceived, and that you - you alone - are the true *recipient of eternal truths.* What will all these others lose by being wrong? NOTHING! Not one thing! There will be nothing, nor any remembrance of anything if you're right.

But on the other hand, what if it turns out that these millions have been right, that God does exist - that His Word is true, that His penalties are just and sure, as He has outlined in the Scriptures? What will you have to lose then? EVERYTHING! You will have sold the south 40 acres for a bucket of unhatched worms. You've acted the

fool and you've had it for all eternity! And you will reap all the penalties revealed by a just and holy God. Even a poker faced professional gambler wouldn't touch a bet like this with a ten foot pole; with stakes this high and odds this poor. So, really, you're not even being a very smart gambler. How can one be assured of and find that goal of eternal life, that lies just beyond this present existence? Surely not by relying on the guesses of another created entity like yourself!

GOD HAS PROVIDED

If we only stop to think about it, our next breath, our next heart beat, and the one we just had, were not produced by us, but they were *provided* to us. Our life functions are something we cannot control to ensure their continued existence. Life then, when fully understood becomes a precious gift! As we look around and survey all our blessings we soon find the really important things have NOT been provided by ourselves through our own self efforts. It's true, that by working, scheming, and planning, with what already has been provided, we've been able to collect a few unimportant possessions. These, we may be able to use for a few years if our health permits or the loan company doesn't repossess them. In time, these too, will go the way of all material possessions - become rusty, obsolete from disuse, and finally end up in some trash heap, garbage dump, or garage sale.

I doubt if many of us can truthfully and emphatically say, "There is no God!", after surveying objectively and listing the vital things that have been provided for our life and welfare. As we meditate on our own creation and life, and the intelligence required to establish this earth and the universe, of which we all are a part, surely we must agree with God when He says in Scriptures, "The fool hath said in his heart, THERE IS NO GOD!" (Ref. Psalms 14: 1).

If we admit, maybe somewhat reluctantly, there is a God, we must also, with the same logic, admit He is still running the show. I surely didn't crank up the sun this morning and I'm sure you didn't paint the sky black last night. As we take an objective look around us at all the marvels of this wonderful universe, we find that it is indeed beyond human comprehension. We soon observe that all things are controlled and operated by strict natural laws with great precision. Harmony and absolute order are everywhere — except with man; who has been given the power of free choice!

> ***For although they knew God, they neither glorified him as God nor gave thanks to him, but their thinking became futile and their foolish hearts were darkened. Although they claimed to be wise, they became fools and exchanged the glory of the immortal God for images made to look like mortal man and birds and animals and reptiles. (Romans 1:21-23)***

Robots Out Of Control

Let's use a hypothetical example of a robot which we design to be so smart it could think and do, within limitations by itself, without any input from us. We are getting very close to doing this from a mechanical and electronic sense. In fact initial models are already being displayed in various countries of the world. After consulting with other like minded robots, or maybe by its own silicone memory chips *(self will)* this one decides it doesn't need *our* help any longer. It assumes it doesn't need the electrical power cord attached to it that gives it life and light and provides energy for a form of intelligence! It wants to be free to do its OWN thing! And so the mechanical hand attached to its side suddenly reaches out and jerks the electrical cord (life line) from the wall. At the same time its mechanical electronic voice is heard croaking *"I am independent* - I AM FREE AT LAST."

Of course as the designers we know what would happen! The screen would go black and the lights would *go out,* and 'Alfie' wouldn't even have the power or ability to reach out and reconnect his own life line. It would be a useless, meaningless marvel, *incapable* of fulfilling even the smallest of functions it was designed for! All hope of reaching its full potential as designed would be gone. And without reconnection to its main power source it would be destined sooner or later for the *junk heap.* An absurd example, you say? Not if we compare this example with our own life.

FOLLY OF MANKIND

Mankind has reached up as it were by his own conceit and ego (his smarts) and asked *"who needs* GOD?" - even though he was designed and created by God and given life on this earth. He has in essence jerked the life line out from the heavenly circuit by refusing to accept God's directing spirit - His WORD, - His LAWS, - His LOVE. Since Adam and Eve's decision in the Garden of Eden to choose their own knowledge of good and evil, man's spiritual screen has been left blank and black. Man has only been running on self-contained battery power! Using self contained battery packs he's been able to shuffle slowly around the laboratory, keeping busy in a mundane sort of way. But the packs wear out after a few years; 70 or so at the most. So, one by one, we are discarded! Sometimes due to lack of inputs or rationalization we run afoul of natural regulations and laws of the universe and are put in the storage room or wander into the wrong place at the wrong time. We are then destroyed by other pieces of equipment on the loose and out of control. With the main power system off we cannot even rightly *discern* our *true nature* or *potential.* We cannot, on a physical basis, without God's Spirit, discern the things of our creator and designer, God.

> ***The man without the Spirit does not accept the things that come from the Spirit of God, for they are foolishness to him, and he cannot understand them, because they are spiritually discerned.***
> ***(I Corinthians 2:14)***

Oh how we shuffle about in our own righteousness (our own estimate of right or wrong) trying to find favor with a higher power that we know exists, ever hoping for a *reconnect.* But it is all in vain for we can never be accepted nor can we be reconnected to the eternal life line by our own *self efforts.* God knows all too well that with the spiritual power source off we can never, on our own, reach out and plug in our own spiritual circuit.

Since we are left with only a carnal physical body we are drawn as a magnet to the carnal, physical, and pleasant things of the world. In our sad condition we are all destined for eventual death and the scrap heap in God's universe.

So man, with bulging eyes, haughty looks and clenched fist has been deceived and misled by Satan's rebellious thoughts. Seemingly he can't comprehend or understand that he's standing on an earth created by Someone; an earth which is part of a universe so vast that he (man) cannot even count or comprehend the number of pieces. Nor can he fathom the size or scope of it all. Without wisdom from God man cannot even imagine his own beginning, or the 'why' of his present existence. Yet his daily existence which is allowed by a continued, totally involuntary heart beat or breath has to be designed, created, and sustained by Someone.

Man cannot *create* and he can't COMPREHEND all that he finds around him, and he certainly can't *create* or *control* any of the universe that swirls about his head. He can *only* use and destroy what has been provided. He can only, by observation and experimentation, discover a few of the existing laws by which it all operates. Yes, man is a totally *dependent* creature. But he still has disloyalty problems. By Satan's prodding he egotistically proclaims "I am supreme!" "I am the ultimate!" "I shall never die!" But the Word of God says otherwise and our experiences of the past and present reveal a different situation.

> ***The fool says in his heart, "There is no God." They are corrupt, and their ways are vile; there is no one who does good. God looks down from heaven on the sons of men to see if there are any***

who understand, any who seek God. Everyone has turned away, they have together become corrupt; there is no one who does good, not even one. (Psalms 53:1-3)

GOD IS A GOD OF LOVE

But God is a God of love! "For God so loved the world that He gave His only begotten Son that whosoever believeth in Him should not perish but have eternal life." (Ref. John 3:16). Yes, God in His grace and love, has provided for our reconnection, as it were - *our* SALVATION.

> *For God did not appoint us to suffer wrath but to receive salvation through our Lord Jesus Christ. He died for us so that, whether we are awake or asleep, we may live together with him. (I Thessalonians 5:9-10)*

Many people are unable to understand this love of God, His long-suffering and His grace, His unwillingness that any should perish; "but that all should come to repentance and to a saving knowledge of the Lord Jesus Christ."

> *This is good, and pleases God our Savior, who wants all men to be saved and to come to a knowledge of the truth. For there is one God and one mediator between God and men, the man Christ Jesus, who gave himself as a ransom for all men — the testimony given in its proper time. (I Timothy 2:3-6)*
>
> *The Lord is not slow in keeping his promise, as some understand slowness. He is patient with you, not wanting anyone to perish, but everyone to come to repentance. (II Peter 3:9)*

Too often we just simply do not understand the depths of God's patience and long-suffering! God is *not* like man, who is quick to judge and condemn others. He is a GOD OF LOVE! He is a God of MERCY! But he will ultimately have to pour out His wrath on those who repeatedly reject His love and way of life. The spiritual laws must be satisfied and fulfilled as surely as the physical laws of the universe demand compliance.

PHYSICAL LAWS OF THE UNIVERSE

Let me give you an example of how God's physical laws work so we can compare them to His spiritual laws.

If we jump off a ladder or fall from a high place, we are immediately affected by certain physical laws of the universe. We will accelerate at the rate of 32 feet per second every second, according to the established law of *gravity*. Newton discovered this law a few years ago, although it has been in existence since creation. It's a good thing that apples do fall *down* and not up, as we would lose a lot of the harvest. Now this law doesn't hurt us if we fall, as long as we have enough falling room beneath us. But the instant our falling room gets to zero, or our free falling space runs out, we find another physical law of the universe coming into operation which concerns the inertia of two solid objects as they meet.

Perhaps we have long since discovered our physical bodies are not as solid as the earth and not nearly as large or heavy. So here we are in the hospital again, this time with two broken legs and a sprained neck. Others have not been so fortunate! The results of breaking God's physical laws were imposed immediately. Each operated relentlessly in strict accordance with *established principles* without any time delay, whatsoever. CAUSE and EFFECT operated in complete harmony. The laws of nature and of the physical universe which we have discovered, operate with unrelenting effect and without concern for either good or bad results.

LONGSUFFERING OF GOD

And so it must be with God's spiritual law! But thanks to God, the timing of the results are delayed! This difference in timing between cause and effect is the

longsuffering of God. If a lightning bolt penalty had come down from heaven to strike you or me dead when we first broke one of God's spiritual laws, it would have been well deserved. Because having sinned the spiritual law of God demands that "the WAGES (or payment) of sin is death." But the love and grace and long-suffering of God allows us an opportunity to live on for awhile in our *sinful state*. By allowing this, God is giving us another opportunity to repent and *turn* from our evil ways. Finally, after many years, perhaps we too made that decision to accept Jesus Christ as our Savior. This, then, rendered null and void the penalty for those sins that were being charged to our account and, instead, charged them to Christ, who died for us on Calvary's Cross.

Yes, it could have all been over in an instant of time - the breaking of the law and the lightning bolt penalty - and we, as condemned sinners, would have been awaiting the judgment of God. God says, "it is appointed unto men once to die and after this the judgment." (Ref. Hebrews 9:27).

Thus, if it were not for the long suffering and love of God, the population of the earth would be diminished overnight, and soon there would be no living person left on earth, since we all have sinned and come short of God's STANDARD. We should give thanks to a merciful and long-suffering God for allowing us yet another opportunity to repent, as He is allowing again this day.

But there are dangers inherent here, also, as we can soon be led away by foolish human error in believing that there is *no* punishment for sin. So we become defiant of God and puffed up in our own selfish ego, while God is 'long suffering,' allowing us to continue, for awhile, in disobedience to His way. At the same time, in love, He tries to penetrate our thick craniums (where the grey matter is supposed to be at the upper end of our bodies) with the knowledge that His way is the only true way to happiness and peace, and that the penalty for our sins has already been paid. God is the giver of both physical and eternal life! Eternal life is ours, *only by choice,* and only if we follow certain basic steps outlined in the Scriptures.

There is nothing in our present condition that warrants any favor or special privileges from God. He can just as easily speak into existence another creation or another type of life in this or another billion worlds. We read in the Scriptures that Christ *spoke* and the present universe came into existence. Our salvation is also all by *God's* EFFORT. So, it doesn't matter if our sins are big or little, few or many, casual or premeditated, - they are all the same from God's point of view. The life line is still disconnected, the penalty is in force; the condemnation is in effect. The good news is that the penalty for our sin has been *paid for* by Jesus' shed blood. The justification of our sins has been ACCEPTED by a Holy God by the resurrection of Christ from the grave. God has thus *provided* all that is needed for our salvation. He only awaits OUR acknowledgement and acceptance!

> ***His intent was that now, through the church, the manifold widsom of God should be made known to the rulers and authorities in the heavenly realms, according to his eternal purpose which he accomplished in Christ Jesus our Lord. In him and through faith in him we may approach God with freedom and confidence. (Ephesians 3:10-12)***

NONE WORTHY OF SALVATION

The world is full of all kinds of people in all walks of life; living in every conceivable situation with a variety of lifestyles, and backgrounds which have shaped their lives. But not one person, on their own, is doing or is capable of doing anything to find favor in God's sight. It does not matter if you *do* or *do not* have all the so-called advantages of wealth, position, power, family or prestige. ALL have sinned, ALL are equally deserving of the death row penalty.

This includes the oldest grey haired man, the prettiest young woman, the highest paid government official, the meanest and most vile person, the meekest, most honest grandma, the macho student or the playboy jet setter. "The heart is deceitful above all things and desperately wicked; who can know it?" (Ref. Jeremiah 17:9). Somehow we find it hard to accept this evaluation of the carnal, degenerate human heart. Surely there is some good in us that is acceptable to a just and Holy God! *All* of us can't be that bad, we lament!

But God's assessment of our righteousness puts you and me and everyone else on the same level, in the same boat, with the same final sentence hung around our respective necks. So what can we do?

> ***There is no difference, for all have sinned and fall short of the glory of God, and are justified freely by his grace through the redemption that came by Christ Jesus. (Romans 3:23-24)***

Right Steps To Righteousness

We must *acknowledge* God as Lord and Creator and Christ, His Son, as our Savior. Does this sound too unreasonable a demand from the Creator of our own lives and of the Universe? Many argue that as long as we have right thoughts and do the best we can, everything will turn out all right. But, truthfully, I really prefer to believe the God of all Creation and rely upon the words of the One who is providing this life and promising eternal life. Let's not rely on the *wishful* thinking of some created entity, like you or me, who has no idea of what is involved in these great acts.

Many today have this philosophy: Do the best you can - try to do good, be sincere - go to church once in awhile and think good thoughts; everything will be OK. This represents man's futile efforts to again try to usurp God's authority by self-efforts. This is merely wishful thinking.

God through the Scripture says, "Repent, and be baptized everyone of you in the name of Jesus Christ for the remission of sins, and ye shall receive the gift of the Holy Ghost" (Ref. Act 2:38). God simply desires that we submit ourselves in obedience to His established spiritual laws, so that we will not reap the penalty which automatically comes from disobedience. Isn't it about time we find out what the Instruction Book has to say about our daily operations?

"What must I do to be saved," asked the Philippian jailer of Paul and Silas in Acts 16:30. Like an arrow, the words came back, then as now: "Believe on the Lord Jesus Christ, and thou shalt be saved, and thy house."

There are plenty of "good cookies" as we'll call them, who might even go to some church building each week and hear God's Word, who include themselves as having done nothing wrong in God's sight that would be accounted worthy of death. They think they will be favored with preferential treatment because of their attendance. Satan has surely deceived them and side-tracked them by an ego trip of *self worth!*

> ***Who is wise and understanding among you? Let him show it by his good life, by deeds done in the humility that comes from wisdom. But if you harbor bitter envy and selfish ambition in your hearts, do not boast about it or deny the truth. Such "wisdom" does not come down from heaven but is earthly, unspiritual, of the devil. For where you have envy and selfish ambition, there you find disorder and every evil practice.***
> ***(James 3:13-16)***

As long as they exclude themselves and feel God is always talking about someone else they will *never* recognize their own UNWORTHINESS and their own *need* of a guiding Savior. They have been deluded by Satan so long that they *do not* recognize SIN in all its many and subtle forms, be it selfishness, pride, anger, conceit, dishonesty, or lack of love toward others. Thus they insulate themselves from the cleansing power of the Word and after a few years even their conscience becomes so hardened that they cannot recognize the voice of God speaking to them. In their deluded condition they will never come to the place of recommitment and repentance which is the first step required to approach a just and Holy God.

Now to you who believe, this stone is precious. But to those who do not believe, "The stone the builders rejected has become the capstone," and, "A stone that causes men to stumble and a rock that makes them fall."
They stumble because they disobey the message — which is also what they were destined for. (I Peter 2:7-8)

They have substituted form and ceremony for a new life in Christ. The end result will be that if they are in the minority they will be miserable and aloof from those engaged in the work of the Kingdom. If they become a majority they will eventually gain control over a specific church and its organization, and eventually they will hire 'teachers with itching ears' - those who teach words they like to hear. Words which flatters their egos - words of love which indicates nothing amiss. Kind words which allow their conscience to again be at ease. But it will not be God's true Word!

For the time will come when men will not put up with sound doctrine. Instead, to suit their own desires, they will gather around them a great number of teachers to say what their itching ears want to hear. They will turn their ears away from the truth and turn aside to myths. (II Timothy 4:3-4)

Since they, then, do not hear the admonishing saving words of Christ they are gradually alienated from the things of God. Their chances of being led to a true repentance for disobedience or to a closer walk with Christ are nil under these circumstances. A gradual separation from the guidance of the spirit to the physical things of the world takes place. A *creeping* paralysis takes over in their Christian walk and in the life of that particular church. And Satan chalks up yet another victory.

But there were also false prophets among the people, just as there will be false teachers among you. They will secretly introduce destructive heresies, even denying the sovereign Lord who bought them — bringing swift destruction on themselves. Many will follow their shameful ways and will bring the way of truth into disrepute. In their greed these teachers will exploit you with stories they have made up. Their condemnation has long been hanging over them, and their destruction has not been sleeping. (II Peter 2:1-3)

JUST MEMBERSHIP - BE CAREFUL

Many of these may have grown up in a specific religion or denomination and have been taught, since childhood, to be good (whatever that means). They soon begin to envision that a few meager self-righteous acts (of their choosing) performed at the right time, or else a refraining from a few specific NO-NOS will assure them a favored position in God's future kingdom. Thus they have become vaccinated by religious activities, by use, disuse, and traditions, and have never really comprehended or rightly understood the true gospel message regarding themselves and the proper claims of Christ on their individual lives.

I tell you this so that no one may deceive you by fine-sounding arguments. So then, just as you received Christ Jesus as Lord, continue to live in him, rooted and built up in him, strengthened in the faith as you were taught, and overflowing with thankfulness. (Colossians 2:4, 6-7)

It is sad to behold but too large a number of so-called

professing Christians seemingly fall into this category of apathy and unconcern. They have become nothing but seat warmers and sometimes complainers, showing no compassion and no love for the lost. Their main concern is how well the preacher did or didn't do. They are so *far removed* from any semblance of discipleship - from becoming a *living* SACRIFICE, that no close comparison to the real thing can ever be made. They are undoubtedly very proud of the fact that their grandparents bought the altar for the front of the church or Uncle Joe contributed the stained glass window for the building. They are equally elated and proud that they have warmed a particular seat for sixty minutes each week in that particular church building. They have substituted a building and pious acts of allegiance to an organization, for real obedience to Christ. In all of these *commendable* acts they have fallen into Satan's *trap* and are totally unaware, and blissfully unconcerned, of their *unacceptable* conduct, as redeemed Christians toward a just and holy God as *revealed* in the *scriptures.*

> ***For this very reason, make every effort to add to your faith goodness; and to goodness, knowledge; and to knowledge, self-control; and to self-control, perseverance; and to perseverance, godliness; and to godliness, brotherly kindness; and to brotherly kindness, love. For if you possess these qualities in increasing measure, they will keep you from being ineffective and unproductive in your knowledge of our Lord Jesus Christ. But if anyone does not have them, he is nearsighted and blind, and has forgotten that he has been cleansed from his past sins. (II Peter 1:5-9)***

I might add an observation that some who fall into this category have grown up in a specific religion or denomination and have been led to believe, by those in control that being religious (by practicing the tradition of their specific religion, as promoted by a specific denomination, individual, seminary or school) they are somehow performing acts very pleasing to God. These actions are *only* right if they reflect obedience to God's Word and the Scriptures which become the check point standard for all actions taken.

This may be all well and good as long as the seminary has taught and the resulting graduating pastors have believed and are teaching the *true* WORD of God. But watch out when this Word is by-passed by TRADITION (rules) of the elders or church fathers, or the "new age" liberal thinkers, as is too often the case.

> ***He replied, "Isaiah was right when he prophesied about you hypocrites; as it is written:***
> ***" 'These people honor me with their lips, but their hearts are far from me. They worship me in vain; their teachings are but rules taught by men.' You have let go of the commands of God and are holding on to the traditions of men."***
> ***And he said to them: "You have a fine way of setting aside the commands of God in order to observe your own traditions! (Mark 7:6-9)***

Leading evangelists of our country have expressed the opinion that on an average only 5% of the membership of any local church are true believers, actually living the Christian life by faith as outlined in the Scriptures! Could this shocking statement really be true? Are only 5

out of every 100 church going people really *true disciples* of Christ? Or does ANYONE who gets in the front or back door qualify? God says "by their fruits you shall know them!" Good question: what fruit are they producing? The question is so vital we must turn to ourselves and ask, are *we* really producing fruit for the Kingdom of God or storing up hay and stubble for a firey judgment for ourselves? We were ordained for good works, not for apathy and unconcern and selfishness.

> ***For no one can lay any foundation other than the one already laid, which is Jesus Christ. If any man builds on this foundation using gold, silver, costly stones, wood, hay or straw, his work will be shown for what it is, because the Day will bring it to light. It will be revealed with fire, and the fire will test the quality of each man's work. If what he has built survives, he will receive his reward. If it is burned up, he will suffer loss; he himself will be saved, but only as one escaping through the flames. (I Corinthians 3:11-15)***

The alternative then is *fruit* that can survive the FIRES of judgment. But if we objectively view our own various activities, indeed, we see something is greatly amiss when compared to the early Christian's walk as outlined.

> ***Examine yourselves to see whether you are in the faith; test yourselves. Do you not realize that Christ Jesus is in you — unless, of course, you fail the test? And I trust that you will discover that we have not failed the test. (II Corinthians 13:5-6)***

If some of today's church buildings are indeed mainly filled up with tares (look alike believers) instead of wheat (true believers) this would account for the confusion, apathy and unconcern for the Word and their lack of spiritual influence in the community. We would probably, also see no evidence of witnessing for Christ, as we would expect to see from obedient believers in the true church of God.

I'm concerned about the look alikes, THE TARES, that Satan has sowed in the midst of the congregations. The tares are described as weeds acting so much like true followers that only spiritual wisdom can tell the difference. Christ warns not to try to separate them for fear of uprooting the true wheat (believers) with which they are so closely entwined. But He promises He, himself, *will separate these* TARES at the judgment and gather them into bundles for burning.

> ***"The owner's servants came to him and said, 'Sir, didn't you sow good seed in your field? Where then did the weeds come from?' " 'An enemy did this,' he replied. "The servants asked him, 'Do you want us to go and pull them up?' He answered, "The one who sowed the good seed is the Son of Man. The field is the world, and the good seed stands for the sons of the kingdom. The weeds are the sons of the evil one, and the enemy who sows them is the devil. The harvest is the end of the age, and the harvesters are angels. "As the weeds are pulled up and burned in the fire, so it will be at the end of the age. (Matthew 13:27-28) (37-40)***

My warning and concern is for the individuals who may have unwittingly placed a church name or building above the *body* of CHRIST, the true church, and for those who follow man-made creeds and *not* Christ. I'm concerned about those who are so close to the kingdom by physical association, yet so far away because they have left the true Word for the traditions of their parents, grandparents, neighbors or leaders. I'm concerned about those who are *not* versed in the Word of God and who are not inclined to take a second look at their situation.

How can there be so many different groups each viewing the acts of all other denominations with scorn and suspicion? Who is right? Are you so naive to think you lucked out with the only right selection? Too often we look for Satan in the wrong places; at the bars and other areas of dissipation and debauchery. But the Scriptures say look for Satan as an "angel of light" in places where we'd least expect to find him. Yes, even in the pulpits of some of our churches where the death, burial and resurrection of Christ is *not* believed or taught. Satan will always be found in places of greatest influence!

> ***For such men are false apostles, deceitful workmen, masquerading as apostles of Christ. And no wonder, for Satan himself masquerades as an angel of light. It is not surprising, then, if his servants masquerade as servants of righteousness. Their end will be what their actions deserve. (II Corinthians 11:13-15)***

I'm sure that Satan has used the tools of division and fear between religions and denominations, to his full advantage as he's divided, conquered and watered down the gospel message. He has used the tool of amalgamation as well. He's joined group after group in ecumenical units, who many times have exchanged the word of truth for the price of union. Satan has indeed had a heyday among the various factors and denominations 'of our day!' Even in the very early church days Paul had to cry out "Are you of Apollos, of Paul, of Cephas or of Christ?" (Ref. I Corinthians 1:12). It is only as we *obey Christ*, not men, he proclaims, will right paths be chosen and victories be won. Today we could cry out with almost the same words - "are you Methodist, Baptist, Christian, Lutheran, Assembly of God, Nazarene, Catholic, etc. - or are YOU OF CHRIST?" There is no other reason for denominationalism and division today except Satan's workings and devices. Just as a bunch of keys in our pocket is testimony of an evil and dishonest world so a world full of religions and various denominations is testimony of Satan's work and success in this arena.

I have a close friend who is a member of a major denomination, who wouldn't be caught dead, let alone alive, in the church my wife and I attend, which is a church of *another* major denomination. I ask, knowing the answer already, who do you feel has promoted such feelings among Christians? If the denominational fathers, then they are the spokesmen for Satan; if from the pastor, then he is the mouthpiece for Satan; if from the individual, then they have been misled by Satan's cunning ways. Satan indeed has to be the prime instigator of any and all such feelings.

CHECK AND DOUBLE CHECK

Please, dear reader, if you are a steady church goer, do not rely on your church attendance record as a passport to heaven. Check your present spiritual status against the written Word of God. Don't check it against my word, or against your pastor's word, or against your neighbor's word - but the true Word of Scriptures. Are you indeed a disciple, a follower of Christ in accordance with Biblical standards? Do you open the Bible each day for meditation and study? Do you spend time each day in prayer? Are you living for Biblical principles? There will be wailing and gnashing of teeth by those who thought they were on the right road but who will find themselves outside.

> ***"Not everyone who says to me, 'Lord, Lord,' will enter the kingdom of heaven, but only he who does the will of my Father who is in heaven. Many will say to me on that day, 'Lord, Lord, did we not prophesy in your name, and in your name drive out demons and perform many mir-***

acles?' Then I will tell them plainly, 'I never knew you. Away from me, you evildoers!' (Matthew 7:21-23)

The Son of Man will send out his angels, and they will weed out of his kingdom everything that causes sin and all who do evil. They will throw them into the fiery furnace, where there will be weeping and gnashing of teeth. Then the righteous will shine like the sun in the kingdom of their Father. He who has ears, let him hear. (Matthew 13:41-43)

I asked a poor lady once (poor in spirit, not in accumulated wealth) what she really believed regarding a specific theological subject. Her answer was that she didn't know too much about theology and she hadn't studied the Bible too much, but that she believed *whatever it was* the church believed in which she held membership. What a TRAGEDY! What hopelessness! What a terrible gamble with one's soul, not to know with assurance, in whom you place your trust for eternal life.

Is this what you believe - whatever some group believes that perhaps by *happenstance* you joined or attend? Or does your faith and walk come from your *belief* in GOD and the promises of his HOLY WORD.

There is one body and one Spirit — just as you were called to one hope when you were called — one Lord, one faith, one baptism; one God and Father of all, who is over all and through all and in all. (Ephesians 4:4-6)

Do you know you are saved because of your acceptance of God's grace that was poured out for you at Calvary? This is the crux of the whole issue at hand. Are you going to rely in self, self righteousness, self works, man-made systems or ideas, or even some religion - or have you come to the source of all *life*, the source of *eternal* LIFE; the true God?

Have you proven to your satisfaction that His word is true and *use it* as your *final* AUTHORITY? Has Christ become the number one source of praise, promise and hope in your life? If you don't really believe the above, it doesn't matter what you believe. You may join any group or activity that pleases you and that makes you feel good for your short stay on earth - whether a temple, lodge or country club. All of these have certain merits and advantages, but not regarding the subject at hand, which is ETERNAL LIFE as outlined in the Word of God.

We are all inherently lazy, especially when it comes to digging out facts for ourselves. How handy it is to turn to others for a snappy answer. *Answers* we get - but the *truth* sometimes is far removed.

As we tune the TV for a news broadcast we can have the world news and facts all analyzed for us in 30 minutes by our favorite, liberal newscaster. Maybe as an individual he or she might not even know which end of a car to put the oil in or when to come in out of the rain. Do we ever question that or are we concerned about any of his or her knowledge, beliefs, or motivations? We may wake up some day, as a country, to find we are the most deceived, misled people of any generation, even with all our sources of news and instant information! You and I are not going to get instant pre-digested basic truth all spliced together in neat convenient 30-minute time slot packages from any network, regardless of the subject! It just doesn't come in a guaranteed package each and every time we listen.

Propaganda, YES; but basic truth, NO!

We must put observances, facts, and data together, mixed with a full measure of wisdom and understanding to ascertain basic TRUTH, be it worldly or spiritual!

If any of you lacks wisdom, he should ask God, who gives generously to all without finding fault, and it will be given to him. But when he asks, he must believe and not doubt, because he who doubts is like a wave of the sea, blown and tossed by the wind. That man should not think he will receive anything from the Lord; he is a double-minded man, unstable in all he does. (James 1:5-8)

The same procedure must be followed with SPIRITUAL truths as with worldly facts. God says we must try the spirits to find which one is TRUE by gauging actions, deeds, accomplishments, purpose, and motivations with the Word of God.

For this reason, since the day we heard about you, we have not stopped praying for you and asking God to fill you with the knowledge of his will through all spiritual wisdom and understanding. And we pray this in order that you may live a life worthy of the Lord and may please him in every way: bearing fruit in every good work, growing in the knowledge of God, being strengthened with all power according to his glorious might so that you may have great endurance and patience, and joyfully giving thanks to the Father, who has qualified you to share in the inheritance of the saints in the kingdom of light. (Colossians 1:9-12)

The Word of God again has to be the one and only *standard.*

God is saying that as Christians we should all become *fruit producers* and fruit inspectors. We must be willing to compare the actual deeds produced in our own lives with His written Word. Are we indeed bearing fruit "unto every good work"? If not, why not? We are cautioned, however, never to set ourselves up as a judge of others, on the basis of our own individual beliefs, traditions or likings - or even judge others by the same word of God. God is the sole judge of the intent and motives of each human heart.

> ***So then, each of us will give an account of himself to God. Therefore let us stop passing judgment on one another. Instead, make up your mind not to put any stumbling block or obstacle in your brother's way. (Romans 14:12-13)***

EARLY CHRISTIANS

As one studies the lives of the early apostles outlined in the Scriptures we find that Barnabas and others in the early church sold all their property and brought the money and gave it for the exclusive use and propagation of the early church and its members. They met on a daily basis to praise and worship the Lord, counting all material things in the world as nothing as compared to the riches they had found in the new gospel (good news) of Christ. We as Christians are also admonished not to forsake the assembling or meeting together with others of like mind.

What a contrast this is to us, the professing Christians of this day and age! We are without doubt, as we compare events and prophecies, living in the last church age before the soon return of Christ described in Revelation 3. This is noted as the Laodicean church age. Not only were these actual churches in Paul's day but they represent all the progression of churches during the seven different church periods of the age of grace since that time. The last being the Laodicean church age. Even in this last church age will be found somewhere churches representative of all the church ages - but the predominate or overriding church will be described as Laodicean.

Christ says that when He comes back to earth again He will find little faith on earth! Since faith is a word used of Christians, and not the unbelievers, Christ is undoubtedly referring to the Christian community. The churches, in the Laodicean church age, are aptly described as being rich in worldly goods and in need of nothing, (teaching the tradition of men) but with Christ shut outside the door. But seemingly all are so busy inside (with their own programs and activities) they have not even missed His presence in their midst.

> *"To the angel of the church in Laodicea write: These are the words of the Amen, the faithful and true witness, the ruler of God's creation. I know your deeds, that you are neither cold nor hot. I wish you were either one or the other! So, because you are lukewarm — neither hot nor cold — I am about to spit you out of my mouth. You say, 'I am rich; I have acquired wealth and do not need a thing.' But you do not realize that you are wretched, pitiful, poor, blind and naked. I counsel you to buy from me gold refined in the fire, so you can become rich; and white clothes to wear, so you can cover your shameful nakedness; and salve to put on your eyes, so you can see. Those whom I love I rebuke and discipline. So be earnest, and repent. Here I am! I stand at the door and knock. If anyone hears my voice and opens the door, I will come in and eat with him, and he with me. (Revelation 3:14-20)*

What an accurate description of their man inspired activities as the true Word of God is being rejected and ignored by so many in the last days of this age. Such activity will increase as the final church period draws to a close. You're probably thinking by now what grudge do I, as an author, have against your church! NONE! The church has been and is *God's* INSTRUMENT for presenting the gospel message and bringing salvation to lost souls in this age of grace.

CHRIST IS THE HEAD OF THE CHURCH!

I *love* the church, if you are referring to it as the body of true believers; as an *organism,* and not as a building, or an organization. What is the bride of Christ (the church) that Paul refers to in Ephesians 5:23-27? Can it be an organization, a building, an idea; or is it the corporate body of individuals who have been redeemed by Christ?

TRUE CHURCH

The true body of Christ, the *church,* is an organism of believers *not a man conceived* ORGANIZATION approved by the I.R.S.!

> ***He is the image of the invisible God, the firstborn over all creation. For by him all things were created: things in heaven and on earth, visible and invisible, whether thrones or powers or rulers or authorities; all things were created by him and for him. He is before all things, and in him all things hold together. And he is the head of the body, the church; he is the beginning and the firstborn from among the dead, so that in everything he might have the supremacy. (Colossians 1:15-18)***

What foolishness for us, a member of a particular man-made denomination or religious group, to view with suspicion and scorn all the members of all *other* groups because they are organized differently than ourselves. Do you think their theology is ridden with error? Maybe so - but look closely at home - you may find a few pin holes in your own. Don't you know they are all doing the very same thing in looking at us with scorn, ridicule and suspicion? We're all guilty of taking our few selected scriptures with our own interpretations and immortalizing them as our brand of theology.

Only those individuals who have *named* the name of CHRIST as their Lord and Savior - who have *accepted* the love and *grace* of God and the crucifixion of Christ for their sins - who have *accepted* the ATONEMENT of Christ with joy - who have been washed by the waters of baptism - and who seek and OBEY God's will, can rightly be called the *church,* the bride of Christ. These should all be our brothers and sisters in Christ - not just the members of our own denomination or group. It is wrong to consider even those of our own system or group as Christian brothers if they do not obey and follow the words of Christ in their everyday living.

> ***If anyone teaches false doctrines and does not agree to the sound instruction of our Lord Jesus Christ and to godly teaching, he is conceited and understands nothing. He has an unhealthy interest in controversies and arguments that result in envy, quarreling, malicious talk, evil suspicions and constant friction between men of corrupt mind, who have been robbed of the truth and who think that godliness is a means to financial gain. (I Timothy 6:3-5)***
>
> ***But now I am writing you that you must not associate with anyone who calls himself a brother but is sexually immoral or greedy, an idolater or***

a slanderer, a drunkard or a swindler. With such a man do not even eat. (I Corinthians 5:11)

It behooves us then, if we belong to any church organization, if we have proclaimed the name of Christ as our Savior, to constantly check our Christian attitude toward others and our Christian walk, in the light of God's Word. If after self analysis we find ourselves drifting from the *word* and into the *world*, since our first profession of faith, then ALL IS NOT WELL. Don't ever believe you can do as you choose - regardless of who says it or suggests it. Church membership by letter, as we know and *rely* upon it today, is not even mentioned in the Scriptures, nor was it a part of the early church. Christ is the *central theme* of all Scriptures. He alone is the source of salvation!

See to it that no one takes you captive through hollow and deceptive philosophy, which depends on human tradition and the basic principles of this world rather than on Christ. For in Christ all the fullness of the Deity lives in bodily form, and you have been given fullness in Christ, who is the head over every power and authority. (Colossians 2:8-10)

Maybe you're thinking "I just don't believe that I have to give up all I own to be a real Christian, particularly my physical property; to sell it and bring it for distribution to the church as Paul and Barnabas and others did in the early New Testament church. I'd rather use a letter and do nothing!" Perhaps so - many do. But taking a look at the total spectrum of activities, with the early disciples at one end, where do we find ourselves in relation to them? Too often at the other *far end* of the spectrum! A few cursory examples:

I personally have heard many long and loud arguments about obeying the Scriptures on the following two points, by people of course who have *done neither.* The first regarding *baptism,* by immersion as outlined in the Scriptures, and the second on *tithing* of income. Most respond with vocal and vehement arguments *of logic* to show why they should refrain from these practices. As an interesting observation over the years, I have yet to meet that *first* person who was ever baptised in accordance with God's salvation plan, who has experienced the joys and blessings of that experience, later come around and say, "Oh, I wish I had never been baptised. It just wasn't the thing to do. NO - *not one!*

> ***You are all sons of God through faith in Christ Jesus, for all of you who were baptized into Christ have clothed yourselves with Christ. (Galatians 3:26-27)***

GIFTS
- ✓ CHURCHES
- ✓ MISSION GROUPS
- ✓ ORGANIZATIONS
- ✓ SCHOOLS / COLLEGES
- ✓ OTHERS

The same with tithing! With our good jobs, investments and possessions most of us would be considered wealthy compared to world standards. But, as professing Christians, our giving or contributing attitude, which is really a true reflection of our gratitude and praise toward God, is often miserly and selfishly motivated. We wouldn't ever consider a tithe (or tenth) of our income for mission outreach or church work - even though we know in our heart that God has really provided the total wealth and income we have. God has set forth throughout the Scriptures the principle and blessings that come from giving of tithes and gifts. No one that I know of who has followed this principle has proclaimed later, "Oh, I wish I'd never started tithing. I'll never do it again." NO *not one!* But all continue with these new found spiritual truths and blessings, once they have been tried and tested. Both of these examples, as well as many others, are set forth as instructions and tenants of faith for us as Christians in the Scriptures.

"Will a man rob God? Yet you rob me.
"But you ask, 'How do we rob you?'
"In tithes and offerings. You are under a curse — the whole nation of you — because you are robbing me. Bring the whole tithe into the storehouse, that there may be food in my house. Test me in this," says the Lord Almighty, "and see if I will not throw open the floodgates of heaven and pour out so much blessing that you will not have room enough for it. (Malachi 3:8-10)

SATAN'S OPERATION

Why do we as 20th century Christians seemingly always find ourselves at the far end of the spectrum from those Christians of the early church period? Do you think God's Word isn't as authoritative as it used to be - somehow losing power and strength and urgency with time? No, the answer is Satan! Satan in I Peter 5:8 is described as "like a roaring lion, going to and fro throughout the earth seeking whom he may devour." How? By temptations! HOW? By *little mundane* TEMPTATIONS imposed upon our thinking and desires that finally lead us down the *primrose path!* Nothing at first that's too bad or too big for a professing Christian, nothing to get excited about, nothing too risque, nothing to put us on the alert or defensive as to his scheme; just small everyday practices that finally engulf us!

When tempted, no one should say, "God is tempting me." For God cannot be tempted by evil, nor does he tempt anyone; but each one is tempted when, by his own evil desire, he is dragged away and enticed. Then, after desire has conceived, it gives birth to sin; and sin, when it is full-grown, gives birth to death. Don't be

deceived, my dear brothers. Every good and perfect gift is from above, coming down from the Father of the heavenly lights, who does not change like shifting shadows. (James 1:13-17)

Satan, as we've seen before, is "the prince of the power of the air". He controls through man all the world's systems whether it's entertainment, sports, governments, education, amusements, or the media! He is the root cause of all suffering, wars, destruction and chaos! A story in the book of Daniel (chapter 10:1-21) gives us an insight unto the workings of evil in our world today. This story shows how Daniel had prayed to God and fasted for three weeks, but to no avail. His prayers were not answered! Later while on the banks of the Tigris River an angel of the Lord came to him in a vision and said "Daniel, God has heard your prayer from the very first moment you started praying and set your mind to gain understanding. But the *prince of Persia* resisted me for three weeks and I was detained there until Michael the archangel came to help out. I am come to supply an answer."

From this we can begin to see the extent of the evil hierarchy that is in existence in each country and it's entangling web of influence over the world. Each nation undoubtedly has a powerful *evil* PRINCE over it, probably a lesser official is over each city, small town and province - and under them perhaps scores of others who try to influence the lives of the populace for evil. All areas of culture that can shape the mind of people are thus over-shadowed by influencing evil powers and demons. All this is counteracted by the prayers and actions of Christians and the angelic army of God. What helpless creatures we are if we have failed to recognize the battle that is raging around us, the character of the enemy, or the methods of spiritual warfare.

Undoubtedly Khoemini and Hitler and past and present rulers in Persia (Iran) and Germany have been and are now directly guided by an evil prince operating under Satan's ruthless schemes. All other countries are influenced as well.

Where the power of the Holy Spirit is severely restricted, due to vast numbers of unregenerate peoples and to Satan's almost total domination of the people, you will always find mass murders, arrests, tortures and concentration camps in abundance. This lack of concern for human suffering and human life will be all too commonplace as no compassion or love will be shown by the leaders in power for those unfortunate people.

PRAYER POWER

Prayers are indicated in this story of Daniel as being answered by a dispatch of angels or messengers of God who bring about the desired results through influence of the minds and actions of others. The more receptive minded, spirit controlled people in an area the easier it should be for prayers to be answered. At least the time

element should be shorter. The more people praying about a subject should also insure a more positive result. Prayers for others, for the salvation of loved ones, sometimes are not fulfilled for years upon end. But if the prayers are consistent, in earnest, and in the will of God, they will in most cases, eventually be answered; as soon as right influences can be brought to bear that will affect that person's life.

What a revealing concept as to the workings and power of prayer. What a need for more fervent and righteous prayers by Christians. We are urged to be instantly and constantly in prayer!

We are urged to pray with all kinds of prayer requests for all kinds of needs; for ourselves, for others, for rulers and governments, laborers for the harvest of souls, for the propagation of the gospel, for family, friends, loved ones, and enemies. The list is long and varied. We must be steadfast in prayer, praying fervently and constantly if we are to be victorious Christians.

> *Be joyful in hope, patient in affliction, faithful in prayer. (Romans 12:12)*

Probably nothing worries Satan or concerns him as much as seeing a devoted Saint on his or her knees in prayer. Have you often wondered why so many distractions seem to come in and rob you of a desired prayer life? Your greatest influence, power, and victories will not come in feverish activities, but in quietness on your knees, communicating with God IN PRAYER.

But too often our motto is why pray when we can plan, worry, or try some other way on our own? In the meantime God is waiting to throw His whole Spiritual resources into the Spiritual battle for us the moment we get concerned and serious about our prayer life. Prayers undoubtedly send into action scores and even hundreds of spiritual personalities in a great *unseen spiritual* BATTLE which rages constantly around us.

CHRISTIANS IN BATTLE

A battle we, all too often, fail to recognize but Paul understood all too clearly.

> *Finally, be strong in the Lord and in his mighty power. Put on the full armor of God so that you can take your stand against the devil's schemes.*

For our struggle is not against flesh and blood, but against the rulers, against the authorities, against the powers of this dark world and against the spiritual forces of evil in the heavenly realms. Therefore put on the full armor of God, so that when the day of evil comes, you may be able to stand your ground, and after you have done everything, to stand. Stand firm then, with the belt of truth buckled around your waist, with the breastplate of righteousness in place, and with your feet fitted with the readiness that comes from the gospel of peace. In addition to all this, take up the shield of faith, with which you can extinguish all the flaming arrows of the evil one. Take the helmet of salvation and the sword of the Spirit, which is the word of God. And pray in the Spirit on all occasions with all kinds of prayers and requests. With this in mind, be alert and always keep on praying for all the saints. (Ephesians 6:10-18)

Paul says we must gird ourselves about with TRUTH. Since basic truth can only be found in God's Word, we will only be able to stand firm with confidence against all evil, as we are fortified and strengthened by the Word of Truth. By putting on the breastplate of righteousness we protect our heart area. This is not our own arsenal of good deeds we are all too willing to pawn - but only that righteousness that God can accept - which must be the righteousness of Christ. For our petitions to be answered we must have a right relationship with God. We will then ask according to God's will - not for our own selfish will. Will it glorify God and build up His kingdom, or help others, or does it promote our own ego and satisfy our own greed?

If we have met these requirements we are admonished to believe by faith that our petitions will be answered. This means having a confidence of the surety of the promises of God's word. Let us never be double minded in our praying, somehow hoping but not really sure they will be answered. But with confidence, resolve, and with purpose present our petitions and desires to God, with thanksgiving, for their fulfilment. God urges us to seek, to ask, to knock and He says "the door will be opened unto us." But none of this will be possible unless we are properly equipped for Spiritual battle.

As we take up the shield of faith we can fend off all the fiery darts and attacks of the evil one. We will then go forth, by faith, in the promises of God and not by the sight and feeling of this world. Satan cannot penetrate such defensive weapons! He cannot succeed against such armor rightly used!

By putting on the helmet of salvation we protect our head, a vital and important part of our physical body, which is also representative of the seat of all physical controls and the governing arena of the Holy Spirit in our lives. We are urged to take the Sword of the spirit which is the only *offensive weapon* we have. With the WORD OF GOD (sword of the spirit) properly used, we can bind Satan and overcome him in any situation.

After being led by the Spirit into the wilderness and fasting for 40 days, Christ was tempted of the devil. Three times He overcame him by refusing his offers. He defeated him by using Scripture; by quoting from the Word.

Few Christians realize the potential power and authority they possess as they allow Christ to come and to abide in their lives. We have the power and authority, in the name of Christ, to bind anything on earth or in heaven.

"I tell you the truth, whatever you bind on earth will be bound in heaven, and whatever you loose on earth will be loosed in heaven.

"Again, I tell you that if two of you on earth agree about anything you ask for, it will be done for you by my Father in heaven. For where two or three come together in my name, there am I with them." (Matthew 18:18-20)

Satan has weakened and deluded us by hiding these potentials from us. The power we rightly have available is the same power Christ has, "As all power is given to Him in heaven and earth."

Then Jesus came to them and said, "All authority in heaven and on earth has been given to me. Therefore go and make disciples of all nations, baptizing them in the name of the Father and of the Son and of the Holy Spirit, and teaching them to obey everything I have commanded you. And surely I will be with you always, to the very end of the age." (Matthew 28:18-20)

He said to them: "It is not for you to know the times or dates the Father has set by his own authority. But you will receive power when the Holy Spirit comes on you; and you will be my witnesses in Jerusalem, and in all Judea and Samaria, and to the ends of the earth." (Acts 1:7-8)

We are admonished to use that power in the present spiritual battle swirling around us. But how few comprehend the BATTLE, let alone the *strategy of conflict* and *the weapons* being used.

If rightly equipped and rightly prepared for battle; by putting on all the spiritual armor available to us, WE CANNOT and WILL NOT be defeated. The resources available to us, rightly understood and used in the spiritual realm, are just too AWESOME for the forces of evil. That is good news!

Thus the initial conversion experience and the experience of living a victorious Christian life (test of our faith) are two interlocking but very separate and distinct phases in the life of any professing Christian. One can be of short duration, the other can take a lifetime.

A World of Testing

EXODUS FROM EGYPT

The story of the exodus of the Israelites, from Egypt, under Moses is a good example of the distinction of these two phases of our exodus from sin and the resulting Christian walk.

The children of Israel had been under bondage of the pharoahs and the cruel taskmasters of Egypt for some 400 years. They had been forced to serve their evil masters from birth to death through many generations.

Even today, all who are still unsaved (in disbelief and disobedience), whose sins have not been justified in Christ are *under* a cruel taskmaster, Satan, just as it was in Egypt. From birth to death they are IMPRISONED in the web of sin and deceit woven by Satan and are influenced and used by him *at his will.* They serve him unknowingly, in some form 24 hours a day with no real hope of escape inherent in themselves. If they suspicion something is wrong, they try to hide, go on vacation, play sick, play church or try frivolous entertainment, but Satan will still be there waiting to manipulate and use them as pawns as it pleases his fancy. He is always watching and waiting for the right opportunity. And he can manipulate them at will, at any time.

> ***Those who oppose him he must gently instruct, in the hope that God will grant them repentance leading them to a knowledge of the truth, and that they will come to their senses and escape from the trap of the devil, who has taken them***

captive to do his will. (II Timothy 2:25-26)

Truly the story of the Israelites' deliverance from their physical slavery is indeed a 'type' of the deliverance of God's people from their slavery and IMPRISONMENT to sin in any age. Moses was called of God while on Mt. Sinai. Under God's direction he went back to Egypt and undertook to free his people by a series of plagues directed against Pharoah and the nation of Egypt. This story is unfolded in Exodus, chapters 3 through 15. After the nation was almost destroyed by these compounding plagues, one last plague of death imposed on all the first-born of Egypt finally opened the way for the exodus of these people from their lifetime of cruel slavery.

Before this last and final plague was imposed God told the Israelites to kill a year-old male lamb as a sacrifice, and to put its *blood* on both door posts and lintel of the door of their houses. *They* OBEYED and as the death angel came through He passed over and spared them from this final plague poured out without mercy on the Egyptians. This action is a reference to and is symbolic of the *blood shed* by Jesus Christ on Calvary's cross for the remission of OUR SINS, as we are justified before a holy God by Jesus's sacrifice on Calvary's cross. The death angel will also pass over us as the wrath of God has been satisfied and removed from us and placed on Jesus by His final and complete sacrifice for our sins and the sins of the world.

> *All of us also lived among them at one time, gratifying the cravings of our sinful nature and following its desires and thoughts. Like the rest, we were by nature objects of wrath. But because of his great love for us, God, who is rich in mercy, made us alive with Christ even when we were dead in transgressions — it is by grace you have been saved. (Ephesians 2:3-5)*

All who accept this sacrifice and grace of God have been cleansed and made as white as snow by Christ's shed blood.

> *"Come now, let us reason together," says the Lord.*
> *"Though your sins are like scarlet, they shall be as white as snow; though they are red as crimson, they shall be like wool.*
> *If you are willing and obedient, you will eat the best from the land; but if you resist and rebel, you will be devoured by the sword."*
> *For the mouth of the Lord has spoken.*
> *(Isaiah 1:18-20)*

The third stage, in the exodus of the children of Israel from Egypt, took place at the edge of the Red Sea. With Pharoah and his army in hot pursuit the children of Israel stood facing the banks of this mighty water; calling on God in desperation at their seemingly hopeless plight. I'm quite sure a few were looking back over their shoulders. As we read we know how God, at night, rolled back the waters of this great river and these people walked across on dry ground out of Egypt to safety. After their passage, and in the morning God let the river flow together again, which destroyed Pharoah and all of his pursuing army. Through the Red Sea, (a type) of baptismal waters, the Israelites as one of their first acts of obedience had stepped out onto new ground in their exodus from slavery (from sin).

> *For I do not want you to be ignorant of the fact, brothers, that our forefathers were all under the cloud and that they all passed through the sea. They were all baptized into Moses in the cloud and in the sea. They all ate the same spiritual food and drank the same spiritual drink; for they drank from the spiritual rock that accompanied*

them, and that rock was Christ. Nevertheless, God was not pleased with most of them; their bodies were scattered over the desert.
(I Corinthians 10:1-5)

GOD'S SPIRIT

Still going ahead and waiting for them on the other side was the presence of God (a type of His Spirit) which led and guided them all the days of their wilderness wandering. This guidance was manifested by a pillar of fire at night that lit up the way and by overshadowing clouds by day.

By day the Lord went ahead of them in a pillar of cloud to guide them on their way and by night in a pillar of fire to give them light, so that they could travel by day or night. Neither the pillar of cloud by day nor the pillar of fire by night left its place in front of the people. (Exodus 13:21-22)

As surely as they were guided by God's presence in these manifestations, so is the born again Christian guided by the indwelling presence of the Holy Spirit, and by God's holy angels. The Holy Spirit of God is again given and renewed in every man, woman, boy and girl who, by faith, has accepted the atoning blood of Jesus Christ as justification of their sins-who have entered the baptismal waters as their first act of obedience to God, and who have determined to follow and obey His Word.

We were therefore buried with him through baptism into death in order that, just as Christ was raised from the dead through the glory of the Father, we too may live a new life.

If we have been united with him in his death, we will certainly also be united with him in his resurrection. For we know that our old self was crucified with him so that the body of sin might be rendered powerless,that we should no longer be slaves to sin — because anyone who has died has been freed from sin. (Romans 6:4-7)

They have become recipients of the Holy Spirit who will guide and direct their future walk and wanderings in this world, if they will but follow!

You, however, are controlled not by the sinful nature but by the Spirit, if the Spirit of God lives in you. And if anyone does not have the Spirit of Christ, he does not belong to Christ. But if Christ is in you, your body is dead because of sin, yet your spirit is alive because of righteousness. And if the Spirit of him who raised Jesus from the dead is living in you, he who raised Christ from the dead will also give life to your mortal bodies through his Spirit, who lives in you.

Therefore, brothers, we have an obligation — but it is not to the sinful nature, to live according to it. For if you live according to the sinful nature, you will die; but if by the Spirit you put to death the misdeeds of the body, you will live, because those who are led by the Spirit of God are sons of God. (Romans 8:9-14)

And do not grieve the Holy Spirit of God, with whom you were sealed for the day of redemption. Get rid of all bitterness, rage and anger, brawling and slander, along with every form of malice. (Ephesians 4:30-31)

Is this all there is to the story of the Israelites deliverances from sin and slavery - crossing the Red Sea out of Egypt to the promised land? No, not by any means. They still had to endure many long, hard years of testing and wandering to finally reach the land of Canaan, the land of rest and promise. As Christians we may have many years ahead of us before we, too, reach our land of Canaan or the land of promise and rest. Our journey will undoubtedly take us through many dangerous, doubtful, and tempting places.

PILGRIMAGE

Paul has likened the Christian walk as a pilgrimage of a stranger walking through a hostile and evil world, as an ambassador in a foreign land.

> ***But you are a chosen people, a royal priesthood, a holy nation, a people belonging to God, that you may declare the praises of him who called you out of darkness into his wonderful light. Once you were not a people, but now you are the people of God; once you had not received mercy, but now you have received mercy. (I Peter 2:9,10)***
>
> ***Endure hardship with us like a good soldier of Christ Jesus. No one serving as a soldier gets involved in civilian affairs — he wants to please his commanding officer. Similarly, if anyone competes as an athlete, he does not receive the victor's crown unless he competes according to the rules. (II Timothy 2:3-5)***

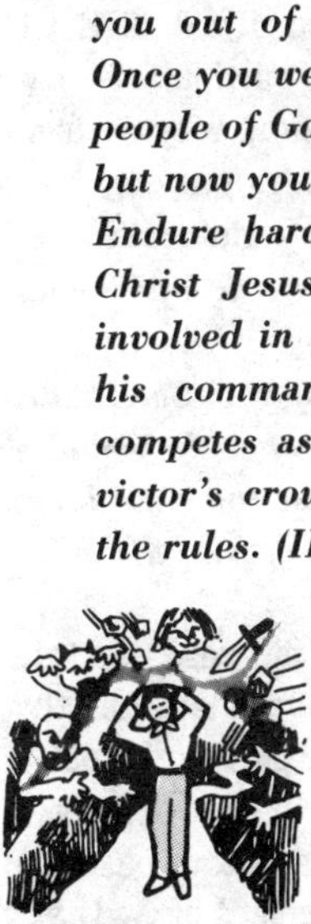

Where in all the Scriptures can you find that this stalwart apostle ever proposed to anyone to sit still, do nothing but wait for the victor's crown to be passed around? Paul thought of the race as a serious competition where many run but few are real victors.

Our human, basic nature is such we always try to find the *easy way* out. If pressures or trials or problems come to us as a child of God we will be quick to change or tone down our Christian walk or witness so we do not offend or cause ourselves unnecessary rebukes and trials. Thus we become afraid of our fellow man's opinion. Yielding to peer pressure we soon become quite useless in witnessing or helping to establish the Kingdom of God. Satan has too often effectively sealed our lips from proclaiming the good news of the gospel to even *one* lost soul. Yet we'll talk about the weather, ball games, crimes, wars, and other people for hours upon end. If trouble starts to come our way we fall on our knees and pray fervently that it will quickly be taken away; that any obstructing situations or people will be *shaped up*. Why? So our way as a Christian, will be made smooth and easy! But Jesus did not promise the Christian walk would be a bed of roses. He promised JUST THE OPPOSITE - one of trials and tribulation, particularly if we take up our cross daily and follow Him. Why is it we spend what little time we do in prayer, praying for a smooth, trouble free life. It's really non-Scriptural.

> ***And you have forgotten that word of encouragement that address you as sons:***
> ***"My son, do not make light of the Lord's discipline, and do not lose heart when he rebukes you, because the Lord disciplines those he loves, and he punishes everyone he accepts as a son." (Hebrews 12:5-6)***

We can only learn to exercise and increase our faith in a *real world* situation. The Christian character that God desires to *develop within* us can only come out of trials, pressures, and testing on this earth - not in heaven. Paul goes as far to say, if our life is a bed of ease and roses, that we are bastards (illegitimate sons of God) and not true sons.

> ***Endure hardship as discipline; God is treating you as sons. For what son is not disciplined by his father? If you are not disciplined (and***

everyone undergoes discipline), then you are illegitimate children and not true sons. Moreover, we have all had human fathers who disciplined us and we respected them for it. How much more should we submit to the Father of our spirits and live! Our fathers disciplined us for a little while as they thought best; but God disciplines us for our good, that we may share in his holiness. No discipline seems pleasant at the time, but painful. Later on, however, it produces a harvest of righteousness and peace for those who have been trained by it. (Hebrews 12:7-11)

Truly these are harsh, unwelcome words to our way of thinking! And how hard we try to twist them around to mean something else, hoping they really don't mean what they say.

Christ personally prayed for his disciples *and us,* not that we be taken out of the world and out of all troubles but only that we be kept from the evil one and not overcome by him while in this world. The next time you find trouble swirling around you, try asking God not only to take it away but to give you the faith, wisdom, and strength to endure and *overcome* it. Your Christian character will then begin to develop in a manner pleasing God.

May the God of peace, who through the blood of the eternal covenant brought back from the dead our Lord Jesus, that great Shepherd of the sheep, equip you with everything good for doing his will, and may he work in us what is pleasing to him, through Jesus Christ, to whom be glory for ever and ever. Amen. (Hebrews 13:20-21)

Brothers, as an example of patience in the face of suffering, take the prophets who spoke in the name of the Lord. As you know, we consider blessed those who have persevered. You have

heard of Job's perseverance and have seen what the Lord finally brought about. The Lord is full of compassion and mercy. (James 5:10-11)

THE UNIVERSAL TEST

The true test of the faith of the individual Israelite came *after* leaving the land of Egypt! The true test of the faith of a professing Christian comes in exactly the same way. Too many of us wish to stop and rest as soon as we've crossed the first river. And far too many do! At this point we may continue living just as the world does, thinking somehow we have been instantly and fully delivered to the promised land. We feel that since we have our own eternal security insurance policy in our back pocket, we can sit back and watch the world go by, having no love, compassion, or concern for lost souls or the admonitions of Christ. We may have developed a smugness that now we have *it made* and are really much better than most others or at least we can transgress with impunity. If this is your feeling let me be the second to inform you, regardless of the implied teaching of some, (and the false hope of all of like mind who do not want to obey or believe all of God's Word) that you've missed an important turn in the road somewhere. Go back to the big "red arrow".

These are not the actions or the hallmark of a truly repentant, born-again Christian. And if you survey the word of God in the Scriptures on this subject, in each and every case, you will find that a Christian's action, walk, and talk will fit within a certain specified framework. It is not business as usual and heaven too! The Christian's life will produce consistent and recognizable fruit! This being love, joy, peace, long suffering,

gentleness, meekness, goodness, faith and temperance.

But the fruit of the Spirit is love, joy, peace, patience, kindness, goodness, faithfulness, gentleness and self-control. Against such things there is no law. Those who belong to Christ Jesus have crucified the sinful nature with its passions and desires. (Galatians 5:22-24)

If you see bad fruit being produced you can be sure the tree is bad and is marked for burning.

> *Likewise every good tree bears good fruit, but a bad tree bears bad fruit. A good tree cannot bear bad fruit, and a bad tree cannot bear good fruit. Every tree that does not bear good fruit is cut down and thrown into the fire. Thus, by their fruit you will recognize them. (Matthew 7:17-20)*

The love of God always is reaching out, always concerned for lost souls and so will we, if we have His Spirit within. If bad fruit is being produced in our lives, then there is another spirit involved somewhere, rather than the Holy Spirit.

> *Dear friends, do not believe every spirit, but test the spirits to see whether they are from God, because many false prophets have gone out into the world. This is how you can recognize the Spirit of God: Every spirit that acknowledges that Jesus Christ has come in the flesh is from God, but every spirit that does not acknowledge Jesus is not from God. This is the spirit of the antichrist, which you have heard is coming and even now is already in the world. (I John 4:1-3)*

We can continue to cling to our favorite pew and the five-minute one-time emotional experience we have had, perhaps long years ago. But if the expected changes that are so necessary have NOT shown up in our life, there's bound to be some misplaced visas when we show up at the gates of Paradise. If this is our situation, let's go searching for the root cause. Let's not leave one stone unturned until we again find that close fellowship and companionship with God that will be reflected *outwardly* as a witness for all to note in our daily walk.

> ***Dear children, do not let anyone lead you astray. He who does what is right is righteous, just as he is righteous. He who does what is sinful is of the devil, because the devil has been sinning from the beginning. The reason the Son of God appeared was to destroy the devil's work. No one who is born of God will continue to sin, because God's seed remains in him; he cannot go on sinning, because he has been born of God. This is how we know who the children of God are and who the children of the devil are: Anyone who does not do what is right is not a child of God; neither is anyone who does not love his brother. (I John 3:7-10)***

Are we going to believe God's Word on what a disciple is or shall we write our own definition?

The Israelites, after crossing the Red Sea, had really done nothing more than to get started on their journey at that particular point. Nor have we, at this juncture in our Christian experience, done anything more than just begun our journey. The real test of our professed faith and belief lies ahead. The results of a vaccination are not always apparent on the day the shot is received. To be effective it has to protect us in the months and years ahead.

> ***Therefore, dear friends, since you already know this, be on your guard so that you may not be carried away by the error of lawless men and fall from your secure position.But grow in the grace and knowledge of our Lord and Savior Jesus Christ. To him be glory both now and forever! Amen. (II Peter 3:17-18)***

Someone else, mainly God with Moses' guidance, had delivered the Israelites intact to the far side of the Red

Sea, in spite of much doubt, misunderstanding, fear and suspicion on their part. In a sense they had been freed - freed from the past. But what would their new past look like from that moment on?

Now comes our moment of truth. As redeemed individuals we are now recipients of the Holy Spirit as our guide (fire by night - cloud by day). We have been delivered from sin and slavery and bondage into a new freedom. We have access to all the armor of spiritual warfare. The victory over sin and death has already been won by Christ. As a Christian we only have to appropriate the victory by living in obedience to the Word - while residing in a sinful and tempting world (or wilderness).

> ***What then? Shall we sin because we are not under law, but under grace? By no means! Don't you know that when you offer yourselves to someone to obey him as slaves, you are slaves to the one whom you obey — whether you are slaves to sin, which leads to death, or to obedience, which leads to righteousness? But thanks be to God that, though you used to be slaves to sin, you wholeheartedly obeyed the form of teaching to which you were entrusted. You have been set free from sin and have become slaves to righteousness. (Romans 6:15-18)***

The all important question for us is this. With all this grace, love and guidance poured out upon us are we *now willing* to continue TO OBEY and follow God's way? It seems to me our actions at this point, if negative, are a far worse rejection than if our refusal had been before initially knowing the Word and the love, power, and grace of God.

The Word of God and His spiritual laws are available to us. We have been delivered from a life of sin and IMPRISONMENT. The Holy Spirit has been given for our guidance and help for our future walk. Do we now cast aside all the grace and love and helps placed at our disposal, and grieve the Holy Spirit or do we step out and claim the victory that is already ours for the asking? Christ knows our temptations and problems and wants to be our great High Priest. We have been forewarned and we have been armed for the battle.

> ***For this reason I kneel before the Father, from whom his whole family in heaven and on earth derives its name. I pray that out of his glorious riches he may strengthen you with power through his Spirit in your inner being, so that Christ may dwell in your hearts through faith. And I pray that you, being rooted and established in love, may have power, together with all the saints, to grasp how wide and long and high and deep is the love of Christ, and to know this love that surpasses knowledge — that you may be filled to the measure of all the fullness of God. (Ephesians 3:14-19)***

TEST RESULTS

How did the Israelites do on this score? TERRIBLY! Only Joshua and Caleb made it to Canaan some 40 years later. Even Moses, because of his refusal to obey God in ALL the details was not allowed to go over *physically* and possess the promised land, but was merely allowed to gaze upon it from across the Jordan river. Centuries later, in the time of Jesus, we do find in Scripiture a description of this great Patriarch standing on the Mt. of Transfiguration with Jesus and Elijah in his transfigured body.

That initial generation of people under Moses grumbled, complained, doubted, disobeyed and were filled with unbelief, even though they were guided, watered, fed and cared for by God for some 40 years in the harsh wilderness of the Arabian peninsula.

That generation *did not* enter into the promised land but they ALL died or were killed! Think of the missed opportunities due to their selfishness and unbelief. Had they only known that by exercising their faith in obeying, and by using the grace and helps bestowed by a loving God they could have entered into Canaan within 40 *days* of their exodus from Egypt.

Christian friend have *you* been doing some *wilderness* WANDERING due to continued unbelief and selfishness? Do you feel this story is *not* given for *our* admonition and that it is not a type or example of *our* Christian walk? Do you really believe a professing Christian can grumble, complain, be filled with unbelief, doubt or ignore the whole Word of God - live like the world by enjoying the same luxuries and pleasures as those who know not Christ, exercise no faith, disobey the will and instructions of Christ; and still find God's favor and companionship in life?

Does God still walk with you in the garden in the cool of the morning or has He been calling as He did to Adam and Eve, "WHERE ARE YOU"? Do you suppose even for an instant, even though you may have taken initial steps to flee Egypt and cross over the sea, that under such continuous, rebellious condition that you shall enter into Canaan, the land of promise, when you have crucified the Son of God afresh? Paul doesn't!

> ***It is impossible for those who have once been enlightened, who have tasted the heavenly gift, who have shared in the Holy Spirit, who have tasted the goodness of the word of God and the***

> ***powers of the coming age, if they fall away, to be brought back to repentance, because to their loss they are crucifying the Son of God all over again and subjecting him to public disgrace. (Hebrews 6:4-6)***

Please re-read the story of the exodus beginning in Exodus 3, which is given us as an example and a type of our own exodus from the bondage of sin. Review your own life and then *judge* not others, but YOURSELF! Are you still wandering with the gang in the wilderness on the far side of the Red Sea due to unbelief? Or are you, I trust, like a pilgrim or stranger, traveling through this sin-sick world, headed straight by God's guidance for Canaan land. If it is the former, I urge you to take corrective action *today*. It is never too late to make a decision, a RE-COMMITMENT, to change, to find forgiveness and to reshape - as long as it is still today. Today you can still exercise your voluntary privilege of calling on Christ for forgiveness and guidance. But what guarantee do you have that you, personally, will be alive to say "today", when tomorrow comes? Are you and I guaranteed another sunrise?

> ***See to it, brothers, that none of you has a sinful, unbelieving heart that turns away from the living God. But encourage one another daily, as long as it is called Today, so that none of you may be hardened by sin's deceitfulness. We have come to share in Christ if we hold firmly till the end the confidence we had at first. As has just been said:***
>
> ***"Today, if you hear his voice, do not harden your hearts as you did in the rebellion." (Hebrews 3:12-15)***

PARABLE OF THE SOWER

In the parable of the sower, Christ, in Matthew 13, likens the Word of God to seed sown at random by the sower. The first was thrown on unprepared ground and the birds soon came and ate it. This is a'type' of the Word of God that falls on deaf ears and cannot penetrate the unregenerate human heart because it is so hardened by sin. Satan swoops in and soon takes away the opportunity to respond or to further inquire as to its merit.

The second type of seed fell on shallow soil on rocky ground and began to quickly grow and develop, but as soon as the sun came up with it's scorching heat, the plants had such undeveloped root systems in the poor soil, that they soon *withered* and DIED. This seed refers to those who hear the Word and momentarily stop and consider it's life-giving qualities and begin to grow and change; but they are soon *engulfed* by *worldly* AFFAIRS and the peer pressure that comes from others and the Word is soon shoved into the background, or ignored. These drop back and drop *out!* They wither and die particularly as pressures and tribulations arise in their initial Christian walk.

The third type of seed took good root and began to grow with vigor. Favored with proper conditions it began to grow and to set roots. But, alas, as it prospered and grew, the weeds and thorns also grew alongside and choked it out. This seed refers to those who hear the Word and start to grow but the cares and pleasures of the world also begin to grow and to become *more* alluring and enticing. As riches and material blessings increase, perhaps from the initial blessings of God, they begin to succumb to an easier life-style until finally the Word (sown seed) is choked out entirely, as the Scriptures say: "by the fast growing weeds and thorns sown by the enemy, Satan."

The fourth and victorious seeds were those which took root in good soil, resisted the pressures and riches of surrounding environment, and produced a harvest of up to a HUNDRED FOLD. This type of seed is he that heareth the Word of God and understands and takes heed and begins to reap the blessings of God and to produce a harvest of souls.

Let's hazard a guess as to which of the four types of seed that Satan is most concerned about and probably spends more time and effort in destroying. It is surely not the first. The first group is already in his camp and only a little divisive scattering effort is required to keep them there. It can't be the second group of seeds because they *soon* wither from a little pressure and heat and blow away. It is surely not the last group, although they can cause him the most trouble. Those who are hidden in Christ, are a lost cause as far as Satan is concerned as they have already found the secret and the power and *moved beyond* his reach. He will try, however, to stop their future good harvest by hindering and stopping their proposed obedience to Christ.

> ***Be self-controlled and alert. Your enemy the devil prowls around like a roaring lion looking for someone to devour. Resist him, standing firm in the faith, because you know that your brothers throughout the world are undergoing the same kind of sufferings. (I Peter 5:8,9)***

SATAN'S PRIORITY

I'm sure the third group of seed demands Satan's constant and undivided attention. They have already established a good root system, gone beyond the initial development stage and have the potential, if not stopped, of producing a good harvest. Once a harvest is produced it is too late for Satan. He has to be concerned with the new harvest and the new seed being sown and produced from that new harvest. As a good harvest is produced Satan will use everything in his power to stop continued harvests. Many professing Christians fall into the category of the third type seed. They start out with a real zeal and love for God, and blessings start coming their way, but they succumb to worldly pressures and desires and their first love is compromised.

> ***Listen then to what the parable of the sower means: When anyone hears the message about the kingdom and does not understand it, the evil one comes and snatches away what was sown in his heart. This is the seed sown along the path. What was sown on rocky places is the man who hears the word and at once receives it with joy. But since he has no root, he lasts only a short time. When trouble or persecution comes because of the word, he quickly falls away. What was sown among the thorns is the man who hears the word, but the worries of this life and the deceitfulness of wealth choke it, making it unfruitful. But what was sown on good soil is the man who hears the word and understands it. He produces a crop, yielding a hundred, sixty or thirty times what was sown." (Matthew 13:18-23)***

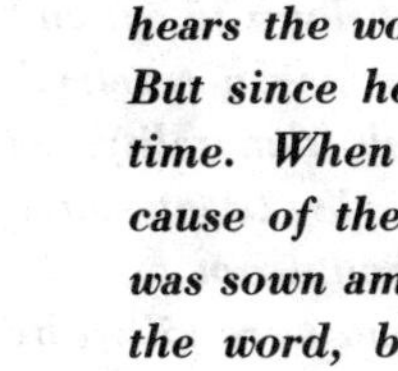

Perhaps they are offended by the Word or its *total claim* on their lives and Satan has them compromise and settle for something less. Maybe they are given wealth and ease of life due to God's blessing being poured out in their life. As a result they become *so*

satisfied after crossing over the Red Sea that they relax and become more concerned with clothes, food, housing, money, land or amusements, than the things of God. Wealth, riches, job importance and security are all leading candidates of God's blessings that can be redirected by Satan to obtain influence and control.

The Israelites in their desert wanderings were always complaining about water, food and conditions, even though God always provided ALL their needs on a *daily* basis. God has also promised to supply all our NEEDS through Christ. Too often we interpret this to mean all of our GREEDS as well.

> ***And my God will meet all your needs according to his glorious riches in Christ Jesus. (Philipians 4:19)***
>
> ***Now these things occured as examples, to keep us from setting our hearts on evil things as they did. Do not be idolaters, as some of them were; as it is written: "The people sat down to eat and drink and got up to indulge in pagan revelry." We should not commit sexual immorality, as some of them did — and in one day twenty-three thousand of them died. We should not test the Lord, as some of them did — and were killed by snakes. And do not grumble, as some of them did — and were killed by the destroying angel.***
>
> ***These things happened to them as examples and were written down as warnings for us, on whom the fulfillment of the ages has come.***
>
> ***(I Corinthians 10:6-11)***

God was grieved mightily by that initial generation of Israelites and only by direct intervention of Moses, on several occasions, were they even allowed as a group to continue to live. At the same time, God vowed that they would *never* enter into His rest.

AND THEY DID NOT!

Lets re-read the story of the Sower again from Matthew 13 and determine from our own actual life style which seed category we really are since the Sower has sown the seed (The Word) in our own lives.

Why would anyone want to wait until the big judgement to find the answer to such a vital question. The issue at stake is eternal death or life! You and I know that after that judgement it will be too late to recover.

If you don't like the looks of your potential seed harvest, I can guarantee that the pains of withdrawal, necessary to affect a change, will probably be worse than those experienced by an alcoholic or drug addict who attempts to withdraw from their addictions. Don't expect Satan to release his hold on you without great opposition. I know from personal experience that you'll only be able to do it with the Lord's help. By yourself, using your own volition, strength or new years resolutions, you will be helpless!

You can only make the change by the same way you initially crossed the river and freed yourself from bondage. This can be done only by the pure and simple *Grace of God*. So you'd better meet Jesus again on bended knee, at the foot of the cross, confessing your worldliness and ask for His help and guidance in restoring your wayward soul.

> ***The Lord is my shepherd, I shall lack nothing. He makes me lie down in green pastures, he leads me beside quiet waters, he restores my soul. (Psalms 23:1-3)***

COME ALIVE AND LIVE

Seemingly few people appreciate the wonderful gift of life itself on earth. What a privilege it is to enjoy the beauty of the day, the opportunity of fellowship, the ability to work, to plan, to just be a separate ENTITY with the opportunity and ability to think, plan and do. Due to adverse circumstances many find themselves bored with their everyday existence. Others are just fed up with all the problems that come their way. Many have experienced set-backs, losses and disappointments resulting in despondency and despair. And without God they have no means to cope! Life on earth for them had become a literal Hell instead of a joy and privilege.

And so without help, without Christ, without hope, many in loneliness and despair have taken the ultimate step of self murder - or suicide. Instead of a solution they have probably found a permanent pit of horror a few years early!

But how many others have chosen a slower but just as deliberate a *death*? They try to deaden their hurts and present existence (in real time) by *escaping* into a fantasy land. How? By drugs, alcohol and other mind warping means. Others try drowning all their sorrow and hurts by pleasures, indulgence and feverish activities, only to find they've compounded them by these very actions.

The older people are always reverting back and talking about the "good old days" where hurt memories can either be ignored or forgotten. The younger generations ignore the opportunities of the present hoping for and desiring the nebulous blessings of future days. Few, it seems, are willing to live life to its fullest in the *only* day we actually can be assured. The only day available is the PRESENT, which is here and now. We, as created beings, exist only in the *real time* world of the PRESENT. So what do we try to do? We ignore the present by looking in either direction to the past or future. Or we try to blot everything, even the present, out of our consciousness.

All events actually take place in what is known as REAL TIME, (the now). All past history is just a series of *present* events that have moved down the corridor of time and into the past. All future happenings will be a series of *present* events that will happen later according to our time reference.

Instead of living to the fullest in the *present*, many who can't escape to past or future, try to fake their way through each 24-hour day by ignoring reality and the opportunities and experience that each moment of time (each second) provides. Some hide in a smoke screen by

creating an aura around them of anger, hate, bitterness and busyness that effectively destroys any potentials that the present might hold for them or any others who might cross their path. People like that can grind up happiness, love, companionships, joy, opportunities, and quiet times as effectively as a six foot garbage disposal on the loose. Do you know anyone like that?

If people can fake long enough (through enough present happenings) they can completely blot out or fake their way through this life. They are not really living, not really enjoying, not making any worthwhile decisions or contributions, but merely existing on hold, until death in some devious form steps in and takes them away. What a tragic waste of a created being - created in the image of God, with opportunity to become a *literal* SON of God. Many of our retired citizens, because they have not known the love of Christ, look only for personal satisfactions and pleasures. They see none of the many ways they can be a help or blessing to others, and so they have in essence placed themselves on HOLD - to wait for death.

This is what this book is all about - to present the OPTION! Life can be satisfying, it can be precious, it can be joyous and fulfilling! It can be worthwhile even on this earth under present circumstances with all its problems, hurts and heartaches! But only if we turn to the ONE, the *only one*, who can give us the peace, contentment and purpose we so desperately long for. That one is Christ, the *Living* Word. Without Him perhaps you've already discovered that there is no purpose to your life and all answers to Life's problems have evaded you. Without Him is the barren hope of man-made ways. Let Christ make your life what it ought to be in the *here* and *now*. Let Him give you the blessed joy and the hope of eternal life for the *future*. COME ALIVE AND LIVE! The God of the universe is waiting to direct your every way.

> ***At one time we too were foolish, disobedient, deceived and enslaved by all kinds of passions and pleasures. We lived in malice and envy, being hated and hating one another. But when the kindness and love of God our Savior appeared, he saved us, not because of righteous things we had done, but because of his mercy. He saved us through the washing of rebirth and renewal by the Holy Spirit, whom he poured out on us generously through Jesus Christ our Savior, so that, having been justified by his grace, we might become heirs having the hope of eternal life. (Titus 3:3-7)***

MAN - A THREEFOLD ENTITY

Since the Godhead is made up of a trinity, Father,

Son and Holy Ghost,it should not be surprising to find that man (who is made in the image of God) is also a *trinity being*. He consists of a body, soul and spirit. Man is not a body - here today and gone tomorrow. Man the entity, simply resides in a temporary, materialist, fleshy body for his short sojourn on earth. He has been equipped with a planet earth body suit. Some of us have been outfitted with male body suits-others are endowed with female body suits. Both are available, however, in all colors, shapes and sizes.

In any discussion on the various temptations that come to man, we must always keep in mind that such temptations can come to us in each of these THREE different realms. And while we may be aware of the dangers and resist in one of these areas, often times we are completely overcome by a temptation that enters through one of the other realms. Although, in a sense, Satan is responsible for the fall of man and his carnal nature, all temptations do not come as a direct assault from Satan. The old saying "the devil made me do it" is not always true in a literal sense. Often man, due to his unregenerate nature, is led astray by his very nature by succumbing to his own lusts and evil desires without any special prodding from Satan or his evil cohorts.

Many times we will find that *one* sin can enter through any one of the three different realms mentioned, depending on the indiviual's motivation for committing that sin. But also, one can be a sin common to all three areas at one time. The most devastating sins that can be committed are those in the Spiritual realm. These are the spiritual sins that are in direct opposition to God and the Holy Spirit. Here can be committed the unpardonable sin of hardening of the heart against the Word of God and blasphemy against the Holy Spirit. Spiritual sins are a direct result of the working and influence of Satan. Satan desires worship of himself - not of God. But even if he has been successful and has alienated man from God, Satan has not always been able to obtain the allegiance or worship *from* man that he desires.

The substitution of humanism for the blessings and love of God is the basic sin of unregenerate people. This is an anti-God religion of setting *self* above God. "Know ye not ye can be like God?" These same words from the garden of Eden are still echoing in our ears today. Any denial of God's working in the heart and mind of man and the substitution of self sufficiency is "HUMANISM." Even though Satan may not always garner the worship he wishes for himself from man in his fallen state, at least he has kept worship from God and may have eternally destroyed the man that God created.

The sins which we are probably more aware of are the obvious sins (or lusts) of the *flesh* (our body). These would include the sex sins of fornication, adultery, homosexuality, drugs, drinking, and anything else that satisfies the lusts of a body out of control. Sins of the *flesh* do not always have to be motivated *directly* by Satan.

Our own uncontrolled lusts often are quite sufficient to accomplish these acts without outside help. Of course Satan can easily set up temptation traps, knowing our weakness and lack of self control in these areas. His temptations then take the form of enticing bait.

The third area of temptation against the trinity of man comes through the area of the SOUL of man. We read in original creation that God breathed into man (into his material body) and man became a *living* SOUL.

He became a *self* entity, knowing and being CONSCIOUS of his own *self* BEING.

The soul of man is controlled by his spirit (either for good or evil) and by the mind of man. The mind of man is higher in order and status than the brain of man. Our brain is merely a living computer taking inputs from the spirit and mind, and transmitting them to the proper body parts for actions. Here input equals output - plus necessary feedback. The brain can be likened to the punch cards or discs that are fed into the computer that allows it to perform directed functions and recall memory information. The brain will die and decay with the body and is not capable of good or evil without consent and or direction from spirit and mind (the Soul). What is fed into the brain is automatically reflected to the body with appropriate feed-back of feeling flowing into the brain and mind. As Christians we are urged to put on the *mind* of Christ; which is the main control area in an individual.

> ***"For who has known the mind of the Lord that he may instruct him?"***
> ***But we have the mind of Christ. (I Corinthians 2:16)***

In the area of the soul probably, unwittingly, are committed some of the more devastating sins of professing Christians. This is the area that is influenced by such outside sources as the way of the world, the pride of life, peer pressures, selfishness, our own personal ego, self satisfactions, and the love of money and possessions. Any of the so-called *good* things of life, if used or treated improperly, or assigned a wrong priority can become awesome sins to a Christian. It all depends on our attitude toward them and how we use them in our daily walk. Read again carefully the admonition of our heavenly Father regarding the love of the *world.*

> ***Do not love the world or anything in the world. If anyone loves the world, the love of the Father is not in him, "For everything in the world - the cravings of sinful man, the lust of his eyes and the boasting of what he has and does - comes not from the Father but from the world.***

(I John 2:15-16)

Once we are aware of the three-fold being of man as areas of potential temptations, we can better be on the alert and offensive in our spiritual battle. Some sins can overlap into all three areas of our being, while others may be confined to a single area of motivation.

As an example, let's take a very practical situation of a young movie starlet or career person moving to a larger city. As a result of circumstances they soon find themselves engaging in sex with their employer or associates. If it is merely a result of the lust of the body the sin could be listed in the realm of a *sin* of the *flesh*. If it is to obtain a better career or more money in their job or to be liked by the crowd (peer pressure), it could be categorized also as a *sin* of the *world*. If spiritually, these individuals believe in their heart that they have no need for God; that they can inheriently substitute their own brand of humanism and acts to get anything a loving God could provide, then the temptation and sin has also moved into the realm of the spirit.

Don't misunderstand me, I am not indicating, under any circumstances, that one sin might be more tolerable or less in magnitude than another, depending on whether it comes from the pride of life (world), the lust of the flesh, or from the direct influence of Satan (spiritual) - but merely to warn that such attacks can come to us through our body, soul or spirit. - or ALL THREE. Sin IS sin regardless of the source. Being forewarned is being fore - *armed!*

Since the spirit is the highest of the control mechanisms in man, we must look to the spiritual area for any permanent desired changes in our actions. To illustrate let's use as an example a car, that at the moment, runs very poorly. It seems on the surface to be in good working condition, but in reality it is so inefficient that it cannot make it to the top of the first hill on the way into town. Under such condition it would be a rather useless vehicle for us to try to use as a dependable mode of transportation.

We have as an option three or four basic areas to initially begin trouble shooting to try to find the basic cause of the car's trouble. It is obvious to all who observe that the wheels are not going around when they should - or they stop when they shouldn't. With this wise observation under our belt do we now proceed to take the wheels off the car and put on new ones, or to change one or the other with a different tire tread? Not likely; particularly if the whole car seems to be running as poorly as indicated. It is true that that lack of right or wrong movements in the wheels are a good indicator that trouble exists, somewhere. It would be foolishness to think *they are the source* of the trouble; or this is the area in which to try to affect a cure of the problem.

So it is with the actions we commit with our body, or the walk we choose to take with our life! We can observe, as well as others, that something is amiss by outside observation; but for the real source of the problem and the cure we have to delve much deeper than what shows up on the surface.

Back to the car again. Do we now replace the drive train such as the clutch, transmission or differential? We surely don't do it if the specific trouble is not indicated in these areas.

What foolishness for us then as individuals to submit to a brain scan or to have a psychiatrist examine our thoughts, or a psychoanalysist to probe our deeper motives in endless sessions when, in fact, the cause of the problem does not lie in any of these areas. Why not go to the real basic source, the main power source - the *spiritual* area of our life and check it out?

In the case of the ailing car we generally head straight for its main power sources - the engine. Normally we begin checking on the primary energy sources flowing into it, such as the electrical and fuel inputs. In 90% of the cases the trouble will be found here! It is quite obvious that since the Spirit and Mind controls the soul, brain, and the body *in that order*, that the mere elimination of a fleshly sin or two at the far end of the cycle will not do much for the overall well being of the individual. But to affect a worthwhile change the Spirit must be renewed (overhauled) - placed under new management. This change made at the source will then properly direct the mind, bringing the soul, brain and body under the righteous control that is pleasing to God.

A few years ago mankind thought that a single cell was just a solid mass of protoplasm, and more recently that an atom was merely the smallest particle in the universe. Now we know otherwise! A cell is a complex living organism of indescribable complexity and the atom houses a miniature universe of electrons and protons and other sub-atomic mysteries.

If in our ignorance we continue to think of ourselves as just a *smart* glob of material (a body) and overlook the fact we are a high order spiritual being, (a trinity) created in the image of God, and housed in a complex body for our short stay on earth; we will indeed miss the mark and the high goal established for us by our Creator.

SATAN'S STRATEGY

The Word of God is the key that can open the door to a new life for any unbeliever. It is also the only tool that can successfully guide a Christian across this wilderness to Canaan's promised land.

How can professing Christians win the battle with the master mind Satan when they don't even recognize him or that a battle is taking place? Many in fact have ignored or thrown away the only offensive weapon in their arsenal, the Word, *(the sword of the spirit)* that can overcome the evil one and the forces of evil.

> ***For the word of God is living and active. Sharper than any double-edged sword, it penetrates even to dividing soul and spirit, joints and marrow; it judges the thoughts and attitudes of the heart. Nothing in all creation is hidden from God's sight. Everything is uncovered and laid bare before the eyes of him to whom we must give account. (Hebrews 4:12-13)***
>
> ***Then I heard a loud voice in heaven say:***
> ***"Now have come the salvation and the power and the kingdom of our God, and the authority of his Christ. For the accuser of our brothers, who accuses them before our God day and night, has been hurled down. They overcame him by the blood of the Lamb and by the word of their testimony; they did not love their lives so much as to shrink from death. (Revelation 12:10-11)***

For all of us who have named the name of Christ as Savior, I would hope that if someone ever lined us up on the church steps and would demand "deny Christ or we'll machine gun you down!" - that under such adverse, tragical circumstances most of us would have harbored the Word in our heart - that we would keep the faith, and be *victorious* in death.

But Satan doesn't necessarily work in such a revealing fashion to alert us as to the true situation. The decision will not normally be so concise and clear cut as to its implications. So we must now "rightly divide the Word of Truth" and hide it in our heart.

(Ref. II Timothy 2:15)

When I was a young boy living in the countryside of southern Indiana, most of the country roads had stone culverts across them to let the small streams or excess

rain water drain off the fields. In the ever present pools of water collected under these bridges could be found two or three large bullfrogs serenely sitting among the weeds. We would cautiously get a pole with hook and line and gently lower all kinds of enticing bait to a point just in front of the frog; all the time being careful to keep completely out of sight. We would entice with crickets, locusts, various and assorted worms, beetles and young sparrows. Finally by experience we learned to tie a piece of red flannel to the hook. Not only would the frog immediately come to life, but actually he would sometimes jump an entire foot to catch the flannel as it came down to him. Many a frog lost his freedom and his life by not recognizing danger in all its subtle manifestations.

DON'T EVER FORGET THIS STORY ABOUT THE FROG!

Because Satan uses the same tactics on the world and on us as Christians. He knows what *we'll jump for* if he keeps out of sight. Maybe he's tried drugs, sex, and alcohol and we as Christians haven't even blinked an eye. The next time he pulls out his more subtle arsenal. If it doesn't work the first time, he tries it *another time* when our defenses are a little lower. If that doesn't work, he pulls it back an tries another gimmick. And if he finds any holes or chinks in our armor (spiritual gaps due to leaving the Word), he can ultimately gain victory and success over us as he attempts to destroy our Christian walk and witness and to cause us to abandon the love and faith we first knew.

They promise them freedom, while they themselves are slaves of depravity - for a man is a slave to whatever has mastered him. If they have escaped the corruption of the world by knowing our Lord and Savior Jesus Christ and are again entangled in it and overcome, they are worse off at the end than they were at the beginning. It would have been better for them not to have known the way of righteousness, than to have known it and then turn their backs on the sacred commandment that was passed on to them.
(II Peter 2:19-21)

It would be hard to imagine how many tons of golden crowns and rewards Satan has taken and stored in his warehouse, that should rightly have belonged to careless Christians; not that Satan has actually gained them, but the individual has surely lost them, regardless.

Check Points and Road Signs

WORLDLINESS DEFINED

Remember Satan will always deceive by things that do not arouse our suspicion and he'll start slowly until we become so engulfed in his way that we slowly but surely abandon the way of God. WORLDLINESS is in DIRECT OPPOSITION to the WAY OF GOD. Any friend of the world, Christ says, is an *enemy of God!* That is hard to believe when there are so many enticing things in the world that draw us like a magnet, such as the lust of eyes, the pleasures of the day and the pride of possessions. We still have to live in the world, but if we are engulfed and taken in by the world systems we are then no different than the unregenerate; those who know not God!

> ***You adulterous people, don't you know that friendship with the world is hatred toward God? Anyone who chooses to be a friend of the world becomes an enemy of God. Or do you think Scripture says without reason that the spirit he caused to live in us tends toward envy, but he gives us more grace? That is why Scripture says: "God opposes the proud but gives grace to the humble."***
>
> ***Submit yourselves, then, to God. Resist the devil, and he will flee from you. (James 4:4-7)***

We must, as disciples, become like those early pilgrims and strangers if necessary, who had their eyes set on heavenly goals as they walked through this world!

Let's take an example of a typical satanic trap that many fall for. A television set in itself is not an evil thing.

It's an expensive electronic marvel. It is like money which is an inanimate object, a medium of exchange which can be used for many things, such as missionary and church work, buying Bibles, prostitution, drugs or hiring a murderer - all dependent, of course, on the user's *choice.* Television is a captivating electronic media which is capable of bringing information, enjoyment, entertainment and evil into our homes. The selection is ours, whether it is (1) educational: the theatre, the travelogue, or science; (2) informative: the documentary or talk show; (3) inspiring: the church service or musical; (4) entertaining: the soap opera, sports, or the comedy. Again it all depends on the user's CHOICE. Albeit, it is not as neutral as money since its secular programming is almost totally influenced by worldly or satanic influences.

Subtly we may initially start out only looking at news broadcasts, with a few entertaining travelogues and then a ball game or two - nothing big or controversial - nothing evil, or too time consuming! These are all good, wholesome events. We deserve a good rest, we tell ourselves and a little time of relaxation after a hard days work. *Right on!* But I wonder who whispered that little gem in our ear that we so readily accepted? Do we begin to detect the red flannel reflections in the screen? By then we find there's a bigger and better ballgame tomorrow night and so we take that in also. And the next! And the one after that! Finally after a few weeks or months we find ourselves glued in a *hypnotic trance* to ALL the games, soap operas, talk shows, third rate comedies and lower rate junk.

All this is to the *exclusion* of neighborliness, family, friends, scripture study, church programs or other real values in life. How many of us are desperately lonely for friends and good old Christian fellowship? This, a flickering tube, can never produce. At that point whether we realize it or not, we are unknowingly and thoroughly HOOKED with *Satan's* red flannel camouflaged HOOK! WORLDLINESS, en mass, has moved right into our front rooms and into our minds!

The probable minimum daily TV viewing time for individuals is now estimated at 5½ to 6 hours. The average for some is as high as 10 to 12 hours a day. Each of our 24 hour days can be divided approximately into three 8 hour time periods of activity - one eight hour period for sleeping - one 8 hour period for working and one 8 hour period for family, eating, entertainment, hobbies, and the like. Do you know how many of these eight hour days you are being manipulated by the TV world; by Satan. At least 274 of these (8) hour days ... in each of the regular 365 days of the year.

If we indeed find ourselves in this situation as a professing Christian, I humbly submit that you and I are just as thoroughly *hooked* as a drug addict that has to have a fix each day to shield him or her from the harsher realities of true life and from the real time events around them. What is the difference? Only the *means* of MIND CONTROL! Your mind, no less! Anytime that Satan can, he will try to take you and me to the extreme, in order to totally engulf us with a new found pleasure or way of life once we have nibbled at his bait.

A balance beam has a fulcrum or pivot point at the center with two equal length beams extending each way. Satan is never satisfied that we have a semblance of a balanced life but tries to move us to one end of the balance beam or the other so that the end we are on will be at the lowest point. I've never seen family members fighting over use of a Bible, but I've heard of some real healthy battles over the weekly TV guide and schedule.

So you are still a good upright Christian, a true *disciple* of Christ - RIGHT? Particularly if you still go to Sunday School and Church faithfully every week for 120 minutes. WRONG! Even if we did not miss a Sunday we would *only* be spending 13 of those eight hour days we talked about in Sunday services each year. These 13 days compare to 274 days for the pleasure of TV alone! This is not a very likely counterweight of time to balance the other end of the spectrum, is it? It does not make for a very balanced life. Not even if we are hoping to pawn off on the Lord some acceptable balance by a counter balancing act of good and bad deeds. This would be like trying to keep the law by our own bargaining effort - trading one for another - which of course will never work. But by making the comparison we can better view the extent of our own true *involvement* in the things of the world and our fuzzy thinking on the subject. Even our wishful thinking on this possibility of counterbalancing good and bad deeds is suspect. A few good events we've selected will never cause some bad ones to be overlooked by a just God. They are still there - standing between us and God.

TV '*wipe out*' is only one of the many subtle, effective tricks of Satan to turn people from the Word of God. Over indulgence, or going to the extreme end of a normally balanced lifestyle, can be devastating, whether the subject is travel, food, property, money, work, sports, hobbies or music. The list is *endless* and varied! All these may be acceptable and proper to some rational degree but NOT when carried to extreme or excess. All are in the wings and are ever ready to march on stage and take over the lives of professing Christians at the slightest opportunity. If we take our eyes off the heavenly goal they will inevitably focus on something more to earth.

WAKE UP CHRISTIAN FRIEND; *you cannot compromise with the world and still be a friend of God!*

> ***But because of your stubbornness and your unrepentant heart, you are storing up wrath against yourself for the day of God's wrath, when his righteous judgment will be revealed. God "will give to each person according to what he has done." To those who by persistence in doing good seek glory, honor and immortality, he will give eternal life. But for those who are self-seeking and who reject the truth and follow evil, there will be wrath and anger. (Romans 2:5-8)***
>
> ***Since, then, you have been raised with Christ, set your hearts on things above, where Christ is seated at the right hand of God. Set your minds on things above, not on earthly things. For you died, and your life is now hidden with Christ in God.***
>
> ***When Christ, who is your life, appears, then you also will appear with him in glory.***
>
> ***Put to death, therefore, whatever belongs to your earthly nature: sexual immorality, impurity, lust, evil desires and greed, which is idolatry. Because of these, the wrath of God is coming. (Colossians 3:1-6)***

If the masses are doing it, don't count on it being right - it is more likely to be '*wrong*'. You CANNOT IGNORE the Word of God on a daily basis and still expect to be in the race of life which Paul outlined so ably in I Corinthians 9:24 and Hebrews 12:1. You probably have already been wiped out and what you are doing is a funny little juggling act on Satan's fence perhaps ten feet inside his property line. What a pleasant side show that must be for him. You can always count on Satan, the original liar, as being a dishonest surveyor if you're trying to fence walk on the property line - if you're trying to do a good deed - bad deed balancing act. If no one has cared enough for you to tell you, let me be the first to share the sad, *sad news* with you right now directly from the Scriptures.

The good news is that you still can regroup - recover - make a midcourse correction and *get back into the race* for life. *The choice is* up to you - it's YOURS alone! It won't be easy. Satan doesn't care how much juggling you do or how many minus or'pluses' you've punched into your calculator. Satan doesn't care how much time you spend thinking about how fine a Christian you are. He just doesn't ever want you to start OBEYING and ACTING like one as outlined in the Word of God. That is a definite NO-NO! Satan will have you living in a dream world of fantasy that will dissolve away like a horrible nightmare or wistful fog. The Lord would have you live in a real time world of actual happenings and events that count for eternity.

You may not like to hear these condemning words so plainly set forth but they are a true reflection of the Scripture. I challenge you to thoroughly search the Word of God to try to find *any other course* of action outlined for a disciple, a believer, a child of God than *total* OBEDIENCE to the Word and SEPARATION from the engulfing ways of the world. You can rationalize and indulge in all kinds of wishful thinking since perhaps you have a church membership letter on file somewhere, but I can guarantee you if you are counting on that, it will never be forwarded to your new address.

Our basic problem, perhaps, is still our disbelief in all the Scriptures, as the Word of God - the *authoritative*

WORD OF GOD.

In the same way, count yourselves dead to sin but alive to God in Christ Jesus. Therefore do not let sin reign in your mortal body so that you obey its evil desires. Do not offer the parts of your body to sin, as instruments of wickedness, but rather offer yourselves to God, as those who have been brought from death to life; and offer the parts of your body to him as instruments of righteousness. (Romans 6:11-13)

As a prisoner for the Lord, then, I urge you to live a life worthy of the calling you have received. Be completely humble and gentle; be patient, bearing with one another in love.

Then we will no longer be infants, tossed back and forth by the waves, and blown here and there by every wind of teaching and by the cunning and craftiness of men in their deceitful scheming. Instead, speaking the truth in love, we will in all things grow up into him who is the Head, that is Christ. (Ephesians 4:1-2, 14-15)

SURVEY OF BELIEFS

In summary let's conduct a little mental survey of some of our present beliefs to try and help us better understand *what* we believe and *why* we believe it.

(I) Do you really believe that the earth with all of its size (some 25,000 miles around), its beautiful mountains, fruited plains, trees, oceans, and all of its some 3 billion separate but integrated and complex life support systems, could possibly have blundered into existence by some accident? Think about it! Especially when we find it takes an experienced and trained master craftsman and designer to even assemble a simple little mechanical or electrical device such as a $10 watch or a $78 TV set. The majority of us don't have the faintest knowledge or the skills that are required by these specialists as they do their job. We simply know enough to turn it on and if it doesn't work or respond to a little pounding, we are stumped. Wouldn't it take a master mind (greater than any man) to design, create and bring the massive and complex earth and all its systems into existence? Has anyone even attempted to create a "test-tube" earth now that we have a pattern to go by?

> ***By faith we understand that the universe was formed at God's command, so that what is seen was not made out of what was visible. (Hebrews 11:3)***
>
> ***By the word of the Lord were the heavens made, their starry host by the breath of his mouth. He gathers the waters of the sea into jars; he puts the deep into storehouses. Let all the earth fear the Lord; let all the people of the world revere him. For he spoke, and it came to be; he commanded, and it stood firm. (Psalms 33:6-9)***

(II) Can you really imagine how a universe, so vast that even with our space craft and electronic searches we still have no means of discovering the ends of it, or how it came into being? Can you really believe that the universe with all of its uncountable tens of billions of suns and planets, (most larger than our own) just sprouted up like weeds in some onion patch somewhere? Or did it take a Master Designer far wiser and greater than man, who can't even create the equipment to look at it all, to bring it all into existence and to keep it in orderly operation?

> ***"Can you bind the beautiful Pleiades? Can you loose the cords of Orion? Can you bring forth the***

constellations in their seasons or lead out the Bear with its cubs? Do you know the laws of the heavens? Can you set up God's dominion over the earth? "Can you raise your voice to the clouds and cover yourself with a flood of water? Do you send the lightning bolts on their way? Do they report to you. Here we are? Who endowed the heart with wisdom or gave understanding to the mind? Who has the wisdom to count the clouds? Who can tip over the water jars of the heavens when the dust becomes hard and the clods of earth stick together? (Job 38:31-38)

(III) Can you really believe that all the intricate and interlocking laws of science and the universe that have slowly been discovered and identified over the years by a few learned men of each generation are all an end *result* of some *uncontrolled* CONFUSION? Man has learned more about universal laws in the last 20 years than he has during the previous 6000 years. What about all the laws which haven't yet been discovered, but undoubtedly will be by future generations? Doesn't this leave man fairly far behind in the basic knowledge and creation department?

I am the Lord, and there is no other; apart from me there is no God. I will strengthen you, though you have not acknowledged me, so that from the rising of the sun to the place of its setting men may know there is none besides me. I am the Lord, and there is no other. I form the light and create darkness, I bring prosperity and create disaster; I, the Lord, do all these things. It is I who made the earth and created mankind upon it. My own hands stretched out the heavens; I marshalled their starry hosts.
(Isaiah 45:5-7, 12)

Where did the space come from in which to establish

such a vast creation as the Universe? What was here before any space? Is the space in which the vast universe exists a *creation* or has it *always existed*? Is space something or is it *nothing*? Can you or I answer these questions? OF COURSE NOT. God asked the same questions when conversing with Job. "Then the Lord answered Job out of the whirlwind, and said, Who is this that darkeneth counsel by words without knowledge? Gird up now thy loins like a man; for I will demand of thee, and answer thou me. Where wast thou when I laid the foundations of the earth? Declare, if thou has understanding. Who hath laid the measures thereof, if thou knowest? Or who has stretched the line upon it? Whereupon are the foundations thereof fastened? Or who laid the corner stone thereof; when the morning stars sang together, and all the sons of God shouted for joy?" (Ref. Job 38:1-7)

(IV) Where did you originally come from - you with this marvelously created body that has the ability to think, choose and change your many emotions? How long are you going to stay here on this planet? Will you be here the rest of the day, tomorrow, next year, or will you be around for an eternity? Where will you go when you die? Man CANNOT answer these questions except as they are revealed to him by the Word of God!

> ***When I consider your heavens, the work of your fingers, the moon and the stars, which you have set in place, what is man that you are mindful of him, the son of man that you care for him? You made him a little lower than the heavenly beings and crowned him with glory and honor. You made him ruler over the works of your hands; you put everything under his feet: all flocks and herds, and the beasts of the field, the birds of the air, and the fish of the sea, all that swim the paths of the seas. O Lord, our Lord, how majes-***

tic is your name is all the earth! (Psalms 8:3-9)

(V) Why did you become a part of a particular religion or denomination that you're now in? Was it because, after a longtime study, you were convinced of its truths? Or was it because of an ad or article you discovered in the paper? Was it because of your past background? Was it because that was the *religion* of the country in which you happened to be born or of the particular town or community where you grew up? Was it because your parents or family were members of this or that group or your grandparents before them? Was it because of a chance contact with a friend that led you to a certain place of worship. Or was it because you just happened to attend a specific school or seminary? Or was it by a logical sequence of inquiry and selection?

WHICH IS RIGHT?

It's pretty scary, isn't it, when we realize that by chance of birth, or family or location or chance meeting we could be on the opposite end of any religion or denominational spectrum? We could be on pretty shaky ground if all our spiritual decisions have really been a result of such second or third hand influences and the fickle finger of so called fate.

> ***. . ."Our fathers possessed nothing but false gods, worthless idols that did them no good. Do men make their own gods? Yes, but they are not gods!" This is what the Lord says: "Cursed is the one who trusts in man, who depends on flesh for his strength and whose heart turns away from the Lord."(Jeremiah 16:19, 20; 17:5)***

Left to chance and circumstance, or the tradition of

man, maybe those now taking communion would have been worshiping man made idols; some could be making pilgrimages to a far away mecca instead of singing hymns in a local church. Others could be visiting a witch doctor instead of a priest. Still others might be cursing, damning or killing members of the other group to which they may have per chance been a faithful member. All this is possible had not circumstances, fate, or chance intervened in our lives in an unknown way! The Christian knows it is God!

> ***So do not be ashamed to testify about our Lord, or ashamed of me his prisoner. But join with me in suffering for the gospel, by the power of God, who has saved us and called us to a holy life—not because of anything we have done but because of his own purpose and grace. This grace was given us in Christ Jesus before the beginning of time. (II Timothy 1:8-9)***
>
> ***Praise be to the God and Father of our Lord Jesus Christ, who has blessed us in the heavenly realms with every spiritual blessing in Christ. For he chose us in him before the creation of the world to be holy and blameless in his sight. In love he predestined us to be adopted as his sons through Jesus Christ, in accordance with his pleasure and will—to the praise of his glorious grace, which he has freely given us in the One he loves. In him we have redemption through his blood, the forgiveness of sins, in accordance with the riches of God's grace that he lavished on us with all wisdom and understanding. In him we were also chosen, having been predestined according to the plan of him who works out everything in comformity with the purpose of his will. (Ephesians 1:3-8, 11).***

Some have said, "It's too complicated, there are too

many voices in the world for me to comprehend. I don't know which ones to believe. I'm going to try to *believe in all of them;* but none too seriously." Others may say, "I'm fortunate, I am NOT going to *believe* in *anything* but MYSELF!" All these still practice a form of religion - and one of the worst kinds which sets unregenerate man up as a god unto himself. With only his conscience or inherited knowledge as a source of wisdom to lead him for good or evil, man is headed for deep trouble. Remember the initial choice in the garden of Eden? What is the right answer to all the muddle and confusion? Is there an ANSWER? Or doesn't it matter just as long as we are persistent in our present beliefs, or unbeliefs, and keep hoping that things will somehow work out as we are kept entertained for our short stay on earth. Should we go back to playing pac-man 24 hours a day, or trip out on drugs, television or alcohol?

BIG PICTURE

If we should get serious about our ONE chance for life and life eternal "where can we be assured," you ask, "of getting right answers"? "You have brought up questions regarding our traditions, our religion and denominations, our pulpits and our belief. How can we know what is right - what actions to take - what to follow?"

If there is one constant basic theme I hope to impart to you, it is this. The Bible is the only true revelation from God the Creator. It and it alone is the only STANDARD or *guide* we have or will ever need. There is no other basis of truth available to mankind!

I urge you to check your religion, your denominational beliefs, your church, your pulpit, your personal beliefs, this book, or any other publication you're going to use. Check its message against God's Word, the only true standard. Since we are beginning to analyze past and present actions, isn't it time for a relook and a review to make sure of right paths?

> *Your statutes are wonderful; therefore I obey them. The entrance of your words gives light; it gives understanding to the simple. Direct my footsteps according to your word; let no sin rule over me. Redeem me from the oppression of men, that I may obey your precepts. (Psalms 119:129-130, 133-134)*
>
> *I warn everyone who hears the words of the prophecy of this book: If anyone adds anything to them, God will add to him the plagues described in this book. And if anyone takes words away from this book of prophecy, God will take away from him his share in the tree of life and in the holy city, which are described in this book. (Revelation 22:18-19)*

First of all if we are interested in the long term results we must get a better overall view of the big picture. To do this we must climb to the top of our mountain as it were, to get away from the forest of trees that block our view, so we can get a better overall view of the surrounding scenery.

When I used to elk hunt in the mountains of Colorado, sometimes 20 or 30 miles from the nearest road or familiar land mark, it was essential to pick out one distinguishing peak on the distant mountain range and take a good look and get a bearing on that particular peak in relation to surroundings. After wandering through the valleys and the unmarked forests without any sense of direction, particularly in a snow storm or on a cloudy day, it was essential to walk to higher ground on occasion, so the surrounding country could be surveyed. If that pre-selected peak could be spotted, then my location could be ascertained and I could proceed on with confidence regarding my general location and direction. How often have I found, to my dismay, that I was headed in the opposite direction than I supposed. To find our way in this life we are going to have to find that standard, that peak, that one Entity, that has a better overall view than we do.

ANY MESSAGES

Have any such messages, for direction or behavior, been left to us or been stuck on the refrigerator door for us to discover? If so and if it is truth, then it must agree with what we see and experience around us. Any objective survey of our surroundings and our universe will be in agreement with the basic truth. They will speak the same universal language. Our input and guidance must come from above and not from the so called forest of trees that surround us. It must come from God - not from any *man-made* god, any *man-appointed* prophet or seer, nor from any member of the human race. Any inputs whether it be from family, friends, neighbors, or groups can be in error. Colleges and seminaries can easily be warped, misguided and misdirected because they are founded and run on man-made inputs and ideas. To be sure of the accuracy of each source we must verify it with the basic foundation of all truth and wisdom - The Word of God.

TRUE REVELATION

To be sure, we must look for the revelation that has come outside of and above the level of our own creation. Some are out looking for spaceships for an answer but no messages of any note have yet been received. Has there ever been any ?

Yes, a large volume of 66 books has endured the onslaughts of armies, wars, persecutions and generations of disbelieving and hostile people. It has survived fires and persecution for millenniums of time. This is the HOLY SCRIPTURES which is still the world's best seller. Isn't that amazing for a book that has been so maligned and attacked? In it is found the reasons for our own existence, for man's beginning and ending , and the overall purpose and plan of God for his creation. It reveals a God that is far beyond any concept of a god we could imagine on our own. It reveals a God who designed and created all things. It reveals a God of unlimited *strength, wisdom* and *holiness,* but also a God of *love* and infinite *grace* who wants eternal fellowship with us, His created beings. It reveals a God that is omnipresent, omniscient and omnipotent.

> ***However, as it is written: "No eye has seen, no ear has heard, no mind has conceived what God has prepared for those who love him" - but God has revealed it to us by his Spirit. The Spirit searches all things, even the deep things of God. For who among men knows the thoughts of a man except the man's spirit within him? In the same way no one knows the thoughts of God except the Spirit of God. We have not received the spirit of the world but the Spirit who is from God, that we may understand what God has freely given us. This is what we speak, not in words taught us by human wisdom but in words taught by the Spirit, expressing spiritual truths in spiritual words. (I Corinthians 2:9-13)***

Can we prove that these Scriptures are the inspired words of such a God? Can we prove that they are indeed divinely inspired and not just an oddball collection of thoughts from men of past generations? Yes, without a doubt, the revelation of God can be proven, verified and experienced as we have previously noted.

> *In the beginning was the Word, and the Word was with God, and the Word was God. He was with God in the beginning. Through him all things were made; without him nothing was made that has been made. In him was life, and that life was the light of men. The light shines in the darkness, but the darkness has not understood it. The Word became flesh and lived for a while among us. We have seen his glory, the glory of the one and only Son, who came from the Father, full of grace and truth. (John 1:1-5, 14)*

GOD'S FOOTPRINTS

But what is so unique about the Bible that it can qualify as the revelation from God? In a nutshell, two things are unique about the Scriptures. First, besides many other things is its *accuracy* in regard to its thousands of prophesies (predictions of events before they happen).

> *And we have the word of the prophets made more certain, and you will do well to pay attention to it, as to a light shining in a dark place, until the day dawns and the morning star rises in your hearts. Above all, you must understand that no prophecy of Scripture came about by the prophet's own interpretation. For proph-*

ecy never had its origin in the will of man, but men spoke from God as they were carried along by the Holy Spirit. (II Peter I: 19-21)

Secondly, its *power* in changing lives.

I pray also that the eyes of your heart may be enlightened in order that you may know the hope to which he has called you, the riches of his glorious inheritance in the saints, and his incomparably great power for us who believe. That power is like the working of his mighty strength, which he exerted in Christ when he raised him from the dead and seated him at his right hand in the heavenly realms, far above all rule and authority, power and dominion, and every title that can be given, not only in the present age but also in the one to come. (Ephesians 1:18-21)

No publication written by man has ever existed that even compares to, or approaches the track record established by the Scriptures.

Some may ask "What is so unique about CHRIST that it proclaims Him the only Savior of mankind when compared to other great men, heroes and prophets of the past"?

Jesus claimed to be the unique *son of* GOD born into the human race with God as His heavenly father. Only Jesus, out of all the other so called prophets of mankind was resurrected from the grave. This event took place on the third day after His burial. After His resurrection He was seen alive on various occasions by at least 500 witnesses over a period of 40 days, before being raised in his new celestial body to sit at the right hand of God the Father in heaven. The Scriptures give us this revelation and the proof. God's revelations are not only unique, but historically accurate as they outline His efforts over the ages to reach down and draw mankind up to Him in order that MAN may have fellowship with Him and become part of the ruling heavenly family.

THE KINGDOMS OF GOD

There are five separate kingdoms in God's created order. These can be shown by illustration arranged in the order or shape of a pyramid, with the different kingdoms representing different layers or levels. First and foremost

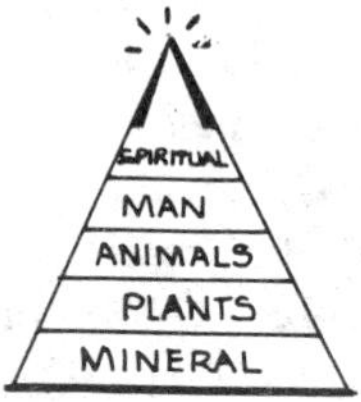

at the apex or peak of the pyramid is the Spiritual kingdom (The God-head). Included here are all the spiritual beings, hierarchies, angels, arch-angels, principalities and powers. For a good illustration of this look at the U.S. seal on the back side of your dollar bill.

Immediately below this level is the physical kingdom of man. Man, we read, being "created a little lower than the order of the angelic host."

Next and below man is the animal kingdom; all the animals, birds and insects that populate the world. Below the animal kingdom is the plant kingdom with all the trees, flowers, plants, shrubs and grasses included. And at the bottom of the pyramid is mineral with its broad base of material, rocks, stone, and dirt that make up the foundation of the planets of the universe.

Seemingly each lower kingdom has a desire to reach up and become a part of the kingdom above it. Its desire probably is to pull itself up to the next level but to no avail. However, each kingdom that is above another kingdom (or level) can reach *down* and use or lift the lower kingdom (in a sense) up to its level.

For example, the roots of the plants and trees go down into the dirt or soil and assimilate it into its being.

Thus, in a real sense, pulling the mineral kingdom up into the vegetable or plant kingdom. The animals eat the plant kingdom and in turn assimilate the plant and mineral kingdom into the animal kingdom. Mankind eats both plants and animals and they are assimilated still higher into the kingdom of man. Mankind, in addition, takes the higher life forms of animals and adapts them into his own lifestyle and habitat.

Now we come to the apex, the Spiritual kingdom of God. How desperately man, the most intelligent creature on earth, with his inherent knowledge of his former unfallen state, has tried over the milleniums, by *self efforts,* to climb up into the kingdom of God. But alas he finds there is *no* way by his own self effort to accomplish this goal. But he keeps trying in every generation. The bad news is that he will never make it - at least on his own.

But the good news is that God is a God of love! Through Jesus Christ He has reached down and has given man a chance to be made a part of (to be assimilated into) the kingdom of God. To become a part of the Spiritual family of God, not in His present form and condition, but by the NEW BIRTH. The consistency and harmony of God's plan is again seen in this illustration.

God's Word sharply contrasts with the writings of men for they all show man's attempt to work, pay or raise his way, by *self effort,* to a higher plain. But with death staring all of us in the face, we can settle for no less a savior than one who has *overcome death* and the grave; for a savior who can lift us up unscathed past this all inclusive *death-decree.* This will be accomplished by a resurrection.

> ***What is more, I consider everything a loss compared to the surpassing greatness of knowing Christ Jesus my Lord, for whose sake I have lost***

all things. I consider them rubbish, that I may gain Christ and be found in him, not having a righteousness of my own that comes from the law, but that which is through faith in Christ - the righteousness that comes from God and is by faith. I want to know Christ and the power of his resurrection and the fellowship of sharing in his sufferings, becoming like him in his death, and so, somehow, to attain to the resurrection from the dead. (Philippians 3:8-11)

All other claims to greatness or goodness from any source are meaningless unless this one point is achieved. No other religion, group or cult can make the historical claims of Christ. Only in the Godhead is eternal existence inherent. So if we wend our way to the mountain top and take a look at the big picture these are the facts we can clearly observe:

THE UNINHIBITED VIEW

1. God is Creator! He created the universe and all that is therein.

In the beginning God created the heavens and the earth. Now the earth was formless and empty, darkness was over the surface of the deep, and the Spirit of God was hovering over the waters. (Genesis 1:1-2)

2. God has revealed Himself through His creation. Thus none are with an excuse.

The wrath of God is being revealed from heaven against all the godlessness and wickedness of men who suppress the truth by their wickedness, since what may be known about God is plain to them, because God has made it plain to them. For since the creation of the world God's invis-

ible qualities-his eternal power and divine nature-have been clearly seen, being understood from what has been made, so that men are without excuse. (Romans 1:18-20)

3. God has revealed Himself to man through His divinely inspired Word.

Your word, O Lord, is eternal; it stands firm in the heavens. Your faithfulness continues through all generations; you established the earth, and it endures. Your laws endure to this day, for all things serve you. If your law had not been my delight, I would have perished in my affliction. (Psalms 119:89-92)

4. God has sent His son, Jesus Christ, (The living Word) as promised, into the world to live, to die for all mankind, and to make atonement for the penalty of sin that was decreed.

Your attitude should be the same as that of Christ Jesus: Who, being in very nature God, did not consider equality with God something to be grasped, but made himself nothing, taking the very nature of a servant, being made in human likeness. And being found in appearance as a man, he humbled himself and became obedient to death-even death on a cross!
(Philippians 2:5-8)

5. Jesus came, lived for 33 years, was crucified and buried; and arose again on the third day.

For what I received I passed on to you as of first importance: that Christ died for our sins according to the Scriptures, that he was buried, that he was raised on the third day according to the Scriptures. (I Corinthians 15:3-4)

6. He now sits at the right hand of God the Father and is soon coming again; this time to rule as Lord and King and to redeem the earth from the curse of sin.

But Jesus remained silent and gave no answer. Again the high priest asked him, "Are you the Christ, the Son of the Blessed One?" "I am," said Jesus. "And you will see the Son of Man sitting at the right hand of the Mighty One and coming on the clouds of heaven." (Mark 14:61,62)

He is dressed in a robe dipped in blood, and his name is the Word of God. The armies of heaven were following him, riding on white horses and dressed in fine linen, white and clean. Out of his mouth comes a sharp sword with which to strike down the nations. "He will rule them with an iron scepter." He treads the winepress of the fury of the wrath of God Almighty. On his robe and on his thigh he has this name written: KING OF KINGS AND LORD OF LORDS. (Revelation 19:13-16)

7. We as individuals can become literal Sons of God (become heirs of the whole universe with Christ) if we accept Him as our Lord and Savior. We will thus be resurrected, given a new celestial body and will rule and reign with Him throughout all eternity.

. . . And from Jesus Christ, who is the faithful witness, the firstborn from the dead, and the ruler of the kings of the earth. To him who loves us and has freed us from our sins by his blood, and has made us to be a kingdom and priests to serve his God and Father-to him be glory and power for ever and ever! Amen.
(Revelation 1:5-6)

How great is the love the Father has lavished on us, that we should be called children of God! And that is what we are! The reason the world does not know us is that it did not know him. Dear' friends, now we are children of God, and what we will be has not yet been made known.

But we know that when he appears, we shall be like him, for we shall see him as he is.
(I John 3:1-2)

THE RESTRICTED OUTLOOK

But as we descend into the forest of trees and undergrowth we still hear these whispers and rumors that Satan and his cohorts of this world would have us believe. They say:

(1) Don't worry, you really can't know how you got here or where you are going, or what the purpose of life is all about! So try to enjoy the interval between birth and death with dissipation and self indulgence. Look to *yourself* and use others of like mind to your own advantage, for all your fulfillments and self pleasures.

(2) Surely this vast creation had to happen by chance, since we proclaim there is no God. This requires that the orderly universe, the beautiful, unique earth, and all created beings, including man, are really just a temporary product of confusion and blind chance.

(3) If you *must be* religious, think up a god of your own imagination; then carve it or make it, the product of your own hands and ideas. Then be sure you fall down and worship it as your god, as your superior.

(4) If you can't stomach that, then accept some man-inspired dead hero or individual conjured up by some group or individuals from a remote past. And then worship that dead being as your holy prophet, allah, or god.

(5) Be sure to set up a system of ceremonies, habits and customs and fervantly keep repeating these until you die. Continue to chant, clap, dance, count, sing, roll bean

bags, beat, kill, drink, abstain, sacrifice, burn incense and candles, whatever appeals to you, to your heart's content. Maybe somebody out there somewhere will hear you or see your fine dedication if you can continue long enough.

(6) Don't worry about standards or morality - enjoy yourself with amusements and dissipation, for if by chance you die you'll know nothing more. Even if you suspicion otherwise just keep on hoping you'll sprout up again in some new form, somewhere else, to start all over again.

Dear Reader, may my prayer be your prayer:

> ***"Lord God, help me to climb to the top of the mountain again, away from the restricted and confusing view caused by my surroundings, and the many false voices around me. Give me an overall view of the true situation! Heavenly Father, give me Spiritual WISDOM and UNDERSTANDING to better comprehend your established ways as outlined in your Holy Word. Open my eyes that I may see - open my ears that I may hear - open my heart that I may receive your Word of truth. In Jesus Name, Amen."***

Some of you, in your present circumstances, if indeed you are behind bars or you have come to the end of the rope, may find these conditions working to your advantage. Perhaps at this juncture in time you are already convinced that so far in life you have indeed failed; at least as far as meeting the requirements of a society or your own version of success. This honest assessment of one's self is very important. As a necessary step of salvation we have to be willing to acknowledge our inability to please a just and Holy God.

The Present Age Of Apostasy

LUKEWARMNESS

God says it is normally the *poor* of this world who will be the ones that are *rich in faith* and who will readily believe the promises of God. The *rich* too often feel they are self-made, some thinking they have become rich by their own self efforts and cunning, and not by GOD'S GRACE. They are satisfied with their wealth, *secure* in their achievements and feel they have no *needs*. They definitely aren't looking and longing for the second coming of Christ when a new order will come and everything will be restored and made new. They are totally satisfied with their present status in life! Their affluent status quo is quite *acceptable* to them. The plight of the rest of mankind, whether in need, in slavery, in prison or in the threat of death, does not penetrate their heart and conscience. Thus, in their present state, they are very poor candidates for "faith," a key ingredient of salvation. Christ had many special admonitions and warnings for the rich and we would all do well to heed a few of them today!

> *Listen, my dear brothers: Has not God chosen those who are poor in the eyes of the world to be rich in faith and to inherit the kingdom he promised those who love him? But you have insulted the poor. Is it not the rich who are exploiting you? Are they not the ones who are dragging you into court? Are they not the ones who are slandering the noble name of him to whom you belong? (James 2:5-7)*

Now listen, you rich people, weep and wail because of the misery that is coming upon you. Your wealth has rotted, and moths have eaten your clothes. Your gold and silver are corroded. Their corrosion will testify against you and eat your flesh like fire. You have hoarded wealth in the last days. (James 5:1-3)

When the young man heard this, he went away sad, because he had great wealth. Then Jesus said to his disciples, "I tell you the truth, it is hard for a rich man to enter the kingdom of heaven. Again I tell you, it is easier for a camel to go through the eye of a needle than for a rich man to enter the kingdom of God." (Matthew 19:22-24)

"Faith cometh by hearing and hearing by the Word of God," we read in Romans 10:17. It is only by our hearing or reading the Word of God that we can ever receive the faith to believe His promises, the facts concerning our lost condition and His salvation offered by the crucifixion of Christ for our sins. It is only by the Word that we read of Christ's resurrection from the grave on the third day. That assures us that we too shall be resurrected to newness of life by the same Spirit within us. Christ is indeed the first fruits of many brethren.

But Christ has indeed been raised from the dead, the firstfruits of those who have fallen asleep. For since death came through a man, the resurrection of the dead comes also through a man. For as in Adam all die, so in Christ all will be made alive. But each in his own turn: Christ, the firstfruits; then, when he comes, those who belong to him. (I Corinthians 15:20-23)

GOD'S WAY - FOOLISHNESS TO THE LOST

"The preaching of the cross," God says in I Corinthians 1:18, "is *foolishness* to those who perish." They will scoff and laugh as the sinners of Noah's day did before the flood.

First of all, you must understand that in the last days scoffers will come, scoffing and following their own evil desires. They will say, "Where is this 'coming' he promised? Ever since our fathers died, everything goes on as it has since the beginning of creation." But they deliberately forget that long ago by God's word the heavens existed and the earth was formed out of water and with water. By water also the world of that time was deluged and destroyed.

But the day of the Lord will come like a thief. The heavens will disappear with a roar; the elements will be destroyed by fire, and the earth and everything in it will be laid bare. (II Peter 3:3-6,10)

Many are called but FEW are *chosen*." (Ref. Matthew 22:14) I'm grieved to read it, but the Bible says only a small percentage of the billions on earth will believe, respond and accept God's great gift. They will *not* believe, regardless of God's Word, the logic, or the evidence seen and observed on every hand.

I must warn you that the same Word will return to haunt you and me. Even though you may not allow the Word of God to take root and save you, it is *all powerful* and everlasting and your refusal of it *does not* change its character or power. That same Word will condemn you and me, justly, at the judgment. At the *judgment*, where Scriptures say, "every knee shall bow and every tongue shall confess - that *Jesus* IS LORD." (Ref. Philippians

2:10-11). This means you and me; everyone of all ages, of every nation will make the good confession. But it will be too late for salvation for the many who have NOT made that confession during their life span on earth while they were still creatures of free choice.

> ***"Turn to me and be saved, all you ends of the earth; for I am God, and there is no other. By myself I have sworn, my mouth has uttered in all integrity a word that will not be revoked: Before me every knee will bow; by me every tongue will swear. They will say of me, 'In the Lord alone are righteousness and strength.' " All who have raged against him will come to him and be put to shame. (Isaiah 45:22-24)***

THERE IS NO ESCAPING THE TRUTH! The true word of God, once you have read it or heard it, shall not return void. And so shall it be this day! It can be a guide to LIFE for those who accept it or a savor of DEATH for those who reject it.

MAN'S ACTION

If you and I are to be saved there is one thing we can and *must do;* and we do this by exercising the power of choice within us. As a first step, as we have noted, we must *acknowledge* our weakness, our failure, our sins and our unworthiness. We will then be able to confess our lost condition in God's sight! Next, we must ask God for His help and then accept His grace and love by accepting Jesus Christ as our Lord and Savior.

> ***"Ask and it will be given to you; seek and you will find; knock and the door will be opened to you. For everyone who asks receives; he who seeks finds; and to him who knocks, the door will be opened. (Matthew 7:7-8)***

Since Jesus comes and abides in an individual only by *invitation,* we must ASK the Son of God to come into our heart and lives. Thus by God's effort in providing and *our effort* in *accepting,* the spiritual lifeline can be plugged into the Godhead, and we will again enjoy the full potential for which we were originally created.

SATAN'S APPEAL

I'm afraid that any refusal to accept God's gift beyond this explanation is not that you and I don't understand the *relationship* and *mechanics* of *salvation,* but that our heart is SO rebellious that we DO NOT really DESIRE any part of God's renewal program.

> ***The Spirit clearly says that in later times some will abandon the faith and follow deceiving spirits and things taught by demons. Such teachings come through hypocritical liars, whose consciences have been seared as with a hot iron. (I Timothy 4:1-2)***
>
> ***See to it that you do not refuse him who speaks. If they did not escape when they refused him who warned them on earth, how much less will we, if we turn away from him who warns us from heaven? (Hebrews 12:25)***

We like to live, with a darkened screen, somehow enjoying the lusts, envy, anger and selfish actions of a lost soul awaiting the coming judgment.

> ***The acts of the sinful nature are obvious: sexual immorality, impurity and debauchery; idolatry and witchcraft; hatred, discord, jealousy, fits of rage, selfish ambition, dissensions, factions and envy; drunkenness, orgies, and the like. I warn you, as I did before, that those who live like this***

will not inherit the kingdom of God. (Galatians 5:19-21)

Such is the true *nature of sin* and the *deceitfulness*, of Satan's control over the unregenerate human heart. Maybe as a first prayer we should ask God to make us dissatisfied with our present walk with the world. Pray that in our rebellion God does not continue to allow us to be deluded in believing Satan's lie.

> ***The coming of the lawless one will be in accordance with the work of Satan displayed in all kinds of counterfeit miracles, signs and wonders, and in every sort of evil that deceives those who are perishing. They perish because they refused to love the truth and so be saved. For this reason God sends them a powerful delusion so that they will believe the lie and so that all will be condemned who have not believed the truth but have delighted in wickedness.*** *(II Thessalonians 2:9-12)*

As noted, Satan is in complete control of earth's systems and as a consequence he controls the mind and lives of much of the population on earth today. Since the fall of man in the garden of Eden, God has allotted Satan some 6000 years of rule over human existence to show the end result of his established way.

We as individuals, and as a collection of nations, are living proof for all the universe to observe that Satan's way WILL NOT WORK! It will be obvious that the way of man, *without God*, will utterly and *totally* FAIL! That man, by his own logic and his own standard, of what is right and what is wrong, or even by his own conscience, will be misled. Don't forget the choice of man in the garden of Eden regarding the tree of the knowledge of right and wrong. Man's way without God will only lead to total *destruction* and *chaos*. This world system under

Satan's control is full of evil, wickedness, lies, deceit and corruption and it will finally *destruct*. We not only find ourselves in this system, but also, too often, a part of the cause and effect.

> ***He will punish those who do not know God and do not obey the gospel of our Lord Jesus. They will be punished with everlasting destruction and shut out from the presence of the Lord and from the majesty of his power. (II Thessalonians 1:8-9)***

THAT DAY

God has outlined in complete detail the end of human effort and governments; the final pouring out of God's wrath on the remaining unregenerate people, and the establishment of God's true kingdom under Christ as "Lord of Lords" and "King of Kings" on earth.

These words are found throughout the writings of the prophets in Daniel, Ezekiel, Jeremiah, the book of Revelation and other areas of scripture. So far, all the prophecies for 6000 years have come to pass EXACTLY as prophesied.

> ***They will make war against the Lamb, but the Lamb will overcome them because he is Lord of lords and King of kings — and with him will be his called, chosen and faithful followers." (Revelation 17:14)***

MAN'S INEFFECTIVENESS

It has only been a short decade or two ago that most people were misled and deceived regarding man's ultimate capability and his ability to solve his own problems

on earth. Science was becoming the great white god and hope of all humanity during this supposed so-called *golden* era. Many church groups falsely assumed that their pious efforts would gradually usher in the promised new age. We as a nation thought we could scientifically create *any utopia* we imagined, that all we had to do was identify the problem, make some grandiose plans, get some free thinkers organized, secure the financial backing, and boom - *instant resolution!* But not any more! It has been said, "The best laid plans of mice and men go oft astray," and particularly of man. Problems are arising faster in the world than we can identify them, or solve them, even with our computers. Man without God's guidance creates more problems than he can solve! The magnitude and number of problems are now so great we hardly know how to catalogue them, and they are compounding!

As this present age begins to close, we can begin to see and to realize the *ineffectiveness* of man as a controlling agency FOR GOOD in world affairs. Man has become the *chief cause* of all chaos and wanton destruction! Only as men are forced or are made willing to be guided by God will proper solutions and right decisions ever be made on earth. Only as God's way is established on earth will lasting peace, harmony and righteousness prevail. Only then will quiet valleys and fruitful plains exist; and love, fellowship, friendship and joy be established for all to enjoy.

> ***And I heard a loud voice from the throne saying, "Now the dwelling of God is with men, and he will live with them. They will be his people, and God himself will be with them and be their God. He will wipe every tear from their eyes. There***

will be no more death or mourning or crying or pain, for the old order of things has passed away." He who was seated on the throne said, "I am making everything new!" Then he said, "Write this down, for these words are trustworthy and true." (Revelation 21:3-5)

Then will the eyes of the blind be opened and the ears of the deaf unstopped. Then will the lame leap like a deer, and the tongue of the dumb shout for joy. Water will gush forth in the wilderness and streams in the desert. The burning sand will become a pool, the thirsty ground bubbling springs. In the haunts where jackals once lay, grass and reeds and papyrus will grow. And a highway will be there; it will be called the Way of Holiness. The unclean will not journey on it; it will be for those who walk in that Way; wicked fools will not go about on it. No lion will be there, nor will any ferocious beast get up on it; they will not be found there. But only the redeemed will walk there, and the ransomed of the Lord will return. They will enter Zion with singing; everlasting joy will crown their heads. Gladness and joy will overtake them, and sorrow and sighing will flee away. (Isaiah 35:5-10)

I'm reminded of the story of the two ants on the log. This was a mighty redwood log some forty or fifty feet long, plunging and plowing through the raging waters - carried out of control by the turbulent, swift currents of the mighty Colorado River. On the back end of this runaway, plunging mass were two ants. Undoubtedly related, as one was heard to say, "Honey, I'm worried!" To which the other replied with much confidence and gusto, "Don't worry dear, I've got my foot in the water and I'm steering."

Even though man has both feet in the water, it is to no avail - he requires his Master Designer, GOD, to lift him up and set him back on the right track!

OUR PRESENT AGE

As evil becomes more rampant, wars and rumors of war will break out on every hand, we read.

> ***When you hear of wars and rumors of wars, do not be alarmed. Such things must happen, but the end is still to come. Nation will rise against nation, and kingdom against kingdom. There will be earthquakes in various places, and famines. These are the beginning of birth pains. (Mark 13:7,8)***

The government of some country in the world seemingly falls from power almost every day of the year. Dislocation of vast numbers of people and mass starvation is taking over from stability and plenty. Refugee camps are now an established way of life for millions of people on earth. *Crime* is *increasing* by leaps and bounds! Riots and confrontations take place in city after city and nation after nation on a weekly basis. This is not a figment of the imagination, or a result of better communications. It is happening!

People are screaming, chanting, shouting in organized and unorganized mobs for every conceivable type of freedom and rights. They want special rights and privileges. They want restrictions to be placed on others. They want to stop this or to start that, when most of the time they do not even clearly know the issues for which they are demonstrating. They are often manipulated by outside interest groups. They form organizations, collect money, and organize mobs to try to disrupt the ongoing society (the established system) and organized business. It's interesting to note here that Satan can *never* CREATE or build up but is always bent on destruction of that which exists. His followers will always follow the same pattern!

The subject matters chosen can range from homosexual rights, women's lib, right to abortion, or the ever controversial nuclear energy problem and the nuclear tipped missile programs.

Yet, property is destroyed, large sums of money expended, both by the participants and the defending society. Arrests and bookings are commonplace as minorities try to impose their will outside the established channels of a working governmental system. The 'big white cause' being proposed in the case of the nuclear controversy is to save mankind from a horrible death, the others mainly involve self rights or peace.

If any of the above individuals or groups were really concerned about human life and suffering and really wanted a better world I could suggest a few other subjects for action. Why not a protest march against alcohol and the drunk drivers which cause such unprecedented *carnage* and *misery* amidst all our lives?

Over one half of the automobile accidents, as documented by insurance companies and police departments, are caused by *drunken drivers.* Over 25,000 people of all ages and walks of life are violently MURDERED on our highways and sidewalks *every year* by drunks. Imagine 70 or 80 lives needlessly snuffed out every day in one country alone! These are not industrial workers working in hazardous situations or military personnel, but the young and the old, mostly *innocent victims,* going about their business of living *until* THE ACCIDENT! Millions more suffer needless injuries each year and many are crippled and maimed for life. The property losses run into billions of dollars each year and the total loss in dollars to our overall national economy is staggering! But who has time to be concerned about any moral issues and their implications?

How important it is for us to clearly get an overall view of the true facts and objectively analyze our own deeds and actions on any subject. When analyzed objectively we find many times the vocal rhetoric we hear is nothing more than a bunch of double talk and does not match the subject or facts. The motives are not even close to what is being said or proclaimed.

The root causes of such demonstrations are generally of a political nature and selfishly inspired. We may find ourselves taking part in the mob scene for another reason entirely different from the real purposes for which the mob is actually motivated. If we are really concerned for the well being and lives of our fellowman, our lives will reflect that concern in the quiet everyday experiences of life, of LOVE and HELPFULNESS to others. You will inevitably find that the LOVE *for God, for neighbor* and *fellowman is scorned* by those who are in rebellion. They will have *no* compassion for others as they are motivated by selfishness and are guided by the great deceiver of this age, Satan.

God has summed up the behavior of such in these last days. "Furthermore, since they did not think it worthwhile to retain the knowledge of God, he gave them over to a depraved mind, to do what ought not to be done. They have become filled with every kind of wickedness, evil, greed and depravity. They are full of envy, murder, strife, deceit and malice. They are gossips, slanderers, God haters, insolent, arrogant and boastful; they invent ways of doing evil; they disobey their parents; they are senseless, faithless, heartless, ruthless, although they know God's righteous decree that those who do such things deserve death. They not only continue to do those very things, but also approve of those who practice them." (Ref. Romans 1:28-32)

> ***Anyone who claims to be in the light but hates his brother is still in the darkness. Whoever loves his brother lives in the light, and there is nothing in him to make him stumble. But whoever hates his brother is in the darkness and walks around in the darkness; he does not know where he is going, because the darkness has blinded him. (I John 2:9-11)***

What an apt description of those in our age we see surging and foaming to and fro like the waves of an angry sea.

SATAN'S STRATEGY

It has been said in a famous quote that if you want to overthrow an empire you should never attack the king - not at first anyway; but it is OK to go after the prime minister and any others on the edge of the kingdom. It is only after you have succeeded in overthrowing all the others that you then go after the king himself. Many are not yet ready to brazenly march against God and His son Jesus Christ in a direct frontal attack. But they are willing to attack on the fringes of orderly governments, the righteous, and the established system of law and order. Once these are brought down, then Satan and his pawns will openly and blatantly attack The King, who he was after all the time. But it will be to no avail as Christ will destroy all of them by His word of command, when He takes over His Kingdom.

Then I saw the beast and the kings of the earth and their armies gathered together to make war against the rider on the horse and his army. But the beast was captured, and with him the false prophet who had performed the miraculous signs on his behalf. With these signs he had deluded those who had received the mark of the beast and worshiped his image. The two of them were thrown alive into the fiery lake of burning sulfur. The rest of them were killed with the sword that came out of the mouth of the rider on the horse, and all the birds gorged themselves on their flesh. (Revelation 19:19-21)

Am I being too pessimistic? Am I drawing on the spectacular of world happenings just to gain your attention? Sorry, but these are facts. This is the true situation we face, the *norm* in the world today, and God reminds us that it will *get worse.* All this is outlined in complete detail in the Scriptures by a God who knows the beginning and ending, even before He created it.

In fact, everyone who wants to live a godly life in Christ Jesus will be persecuted, while evil men and impostors will go from bad to worse, deceiving and being deceived.
(II Timothy 3:12-13)

THE COMING INVASION

This book has been written and published in a country (America) where religious freedom has been available since the founding of the nation some two hundred years ago. Here we tend to think of and relate to other world religions from this exclusive restricted background. As a result the contents of this book has been directed mainly toward those individuals who have, at least, had an extensive background environment of Christianity.

Thus it may be surprising to some to learn that Christianity is in no sense the *dominant* religion of the world. The "Protestant Christianity" label in America cannot lay claim to much over 65% of the local population. If we counted only those who are active in their claims of profession the number would probably fall far below 50% of the total. However in a majority of the other large populated countries of the world these same percentage points would drop to practically zero, or perhaps in most cases, to a few tenths of one percent of total population.

As this age draws to a close, those who believe in the God of the Bible will find themselves *assailed* on every side by these anti-God forces. These represent the various forms of Satanic religion (anti-Christ forces) which will, according to Scripture, hold sway over the masses on earth just before the wrath of God is poured out on unrepentant mankind at the end of the Age.

The disputes and suspicions between local Christian factions and denominations have *blinded* the eyes of most to the real and ever present Satanic dangers. The conflict of political dogmas, ideologies and physical jostlings between governments and nations has diverted the priorities from the true character of these dangers which will always be found in the spiritual realm - not in the physical.

The Christian soul of America is being challenged, invaded and conquered by enemy forces, but few indeed, are even aware of the battle; even to sense the coming tragedy that may be at our doorstep.

Remember the basic and original sin of Satan was pride and the "I" problem. Setting himself up as God! Trying to usurp God's prerogatives and authority! The

basic sin of all humanity through Adam and Eve was their succumbing to the temptation to set themselves up as gods - knowing and deciding within themselves *good and evil!* Believing Satan's lie that they would never die! The true religion of Satan will never change and it can always be identified if we know what we are looking for.

All those who reject the God of Creation and look to *themselves* as the *final* AUTHORITY - who through self-efforts or inner mind power try to manipulate others or things, are the subjects of Satan. As they play with the occult and other mind altering plans and devices such as drugs and alcohol they will be unknowingly taken over and manipulated by evil spirits or demons.

God says in the later days that demonic hordes will be released on the earth and the masses will be deluded into believing the LIE. We here in America perhaps have not yet noticed, due to the restraining influence of the Holy Spirit, what has happened to the enslaved populations around the world. But we will be in for a rude shock and awakening as the Holy Spirit is suppressed and withdrawn due to the sins and evil being committed by the unregenerate, by anti-God people, and yes even by unsuspecting, apathetic, liberal Christians!

> ***The Spirit clearly says that in later times some will abandon the faith and follow deceiving spirits and things taught by demons. Such teachings come through hypocritical liars, whose consciences have been seared as with a hot iron. (I Timothy 4:1-2)***

Don't think that these are all criminals in the sense we might normally use the term. Most, perhaps, are decent, fairly honest, hardworking, socially minded, law abiding citizens; the backbone of society. By their very actions they must be identified as anti-Christ or anti-God in their beliefs. Look around you and you will find a *majority!* Look around the world and this majority becomes an overwhelming flood.

THE ANTAGONISTS EXPOSED

In our count we would have to include all evolutionists, all professors and teachers who teach science to the exclusion of God. We would also have to include all secular schools where the name of God is not permitted, except in swearing. The list must include all humanistic non-Christian psychologists, psychiatrists and doctors. All liberal preachers and church members who have forsaken the Word of God for tradition of men. It would include all those who practice Yoga, use E.S.P., TM, Clairvoyance and Hypnosis, whether it be in kindergarten classes, in police stations, corporate businesses, churches, or at home. Included would be all who read and rely on daily astrological charts. Added to this growing list would be those who use psychedelic drugs or excess alcohol, and those who dabble in the ancient Hindu arts mentioned above. The latter are active candidates for demon possession and mind control. Not control of their own mind but their mind being controlled by other *forces*, be it demons, evil spirits, or Satan himself.

Then look beyond our shores to all the movements and other religions such as Hinduism, Buddism, Animism, Agnosticism, Jainism, Rosicrucianism, Theosophists, Confucianism, Taoism and Humanism and billions more are automatically added to the anti-God fold. Now let's add all the proclaimed atheistic nations (Anti-Christ and Anti-God) that worship only self imposed leaders or rulers, such as the hundreds of millions in Russia and China are forced to do. To these we must also include Japan, India, and Indonesia to round out only a few of the most populous countries in the world.

The *enormity* of the rebellion against God soon becomes obvious. The tides of hell have already engulfed most of the world and the flood gates are already beginning to swing open in Christian America for the *spiritual* INVASION. Did you ever wonder even with all our help and generosity to other nations, why they still hate us so much? To get an answer we must look at a higher level of creation to find the basic cause of conflict, which is Satan's hatred of God and all things of God! We just happen to find ourselves in the front line on this particular battle field.

Yes, this Satanic invasion is taking place by land, by sea, by air and by thought. But the average unsuspecting church attender is content with worrying over the setting of the air conditioning controls or the foam padding on the seats.

The enemy has arrived unnoticed, is active, well, and quickly takes control. This is ungodly rebellion in its very worst form! All these groups, religions, and practices look vastly different on the surface and entirely separate. But not so! They all have one very unifying common ground. They are *all anti-Christ,* they *deify man* or have an open door in some form to occultism or the black arts.

This is Satan's religion that will eventually control the earth in the latter days. It will take very little thinking or changing of allegiance for the masses so indoctrinated, to give full support to the upcoming world ruler - who will be the final embodiment of all their beliefs and practices.

> ***The beast was given a mouth to utter proud words and blasphemies and to exercise his authority for forty-two months. He opened his***

mouth to blaspheme God, and to slander his name and his dwelling place and those who live in heaven. He was given power to make war against the saints and to conquer them. And he was given authority over every tribe, people, language and nation. All inhabitants of the earth will worship the beast — all whose names have not been written in the book of life belonging to the Lamb that was slain from the creation of the world. (Revelation 13:5-8)

Stripped of 100 different coats and a 1000 different colors the core of the basic conflict is thus seen in all its primordial darkness, THE ANTI-GOD FORCES OF SATAN IN REBELLION AGAINST THE AUTHORITY OF GOD!

Maybe you never realized before which side you were really on or perhaps you did not realize a conflict existed. Maybe you just assumed you were in a no-mans land off by yourself somewhere doing your own little thing, OBSERVING the curious activities of others. Such an assumption could not be further from the truth. Perhaps you didn't even realize there was a battle going on. Nothing can be more devastating than being deceived and not knowing you've been deceived.

So which side will you take? Which option do you choose? Which group will you join? The choice, as always, is up to you! But do nothing, and you still will have made a crucial choice.

We are beginning to live in that generation predicted that was "as it was in the days of Noah" before God destroyed the earth and most of earth's population with a flood. Everyone, then and now, wants to *do* his or her OWN THING; without any restrictions or restraints from anyone, not from God, others or society. Thus there will be less concern or love for others as time goes on. We read in II Timothy:

> ***But mark this: There will be terrible times in the last days. People will be lovers of themselves, lovers of money, boastful, proud, abusive, disobedient to their parents, ungrateful, unholy, without love, unforgiving, slanderous, without self-control, brutal, not lovers of the good, treacherous, rash, conceited, lovers of pleasure rather than lovers of God — having a form of godliness but denying its power. Have nothing to do with them. (II Timothy 3:1-5)***

These actions cannot produce peace, freedom or abundant life. They can only lead to anarchy and rebellion, and the COLLAPSE of *civilized* and *orderly* GOVERNMENTS. There must be worldwide law and order for any society, nation, group, or tribe to continue to exist.

SIN ALWAYS DESTROYS

Sin and rebellion flourishes or likes best to operate in a system of law and order where there are restrictions for others but not for itself. People can do their own thing best in an *orderly* society that gives them the *freedom* and *opportunity* to be different and to manipulate and use others. Democracy with its freedoms as we know it can never survive these onslaughts unless a favorable majority of its citizens continue to support and obey Christian principles. Democracy and atheism are in-compatible while atheism and communism are essentially wed.

As law and order is swept under the table, and sin in

all its forms, begins to flourish and take over without restraint, it will soon spiral to destructive power and SELF DESTRUCT. It is like a weather disturbance that evolves during the day from a fluffy white cloud, into a rain storm, then into a raging storm and finally into a tornado that destroys all things in its path.

How could any thinking mind ever begin to rationalize that God could accept such a wayward, sinful, destructive creation into the truly *righteous* and *holy* domain of an infinite God? It would be totally out of place, even in a heaven of man's own making and concept. It would be like pouring together the volatile mixture of oxygen and the chemicals for our rocket engines which explode with fury on contact.

What chaos would ensue in the universe, particularly since everything would be in an eternal existence at that point in time? It is inconceivable, to the mind of any thinking, rational man or woman that *evil* could ever be made an *everlasting* commodity in God's universe. Talk about a *hell!* This would surely qualify as first honorable mention. And how could we expect God to accept this type of action for any length of time even if it were isolated in a remote corner of the Universe, on a planet called Earth? *Evil* only disintegrates into *destruction* and *death* - it does *not* lead to peace, happiness and harmony. It always *self* DESTRUCTS!

> ***Now, brothers, about times and dates we do not need to write to you, for you know very well that the day of the Lord will come like a thief in the night. While people are saying, "Peace and safety," destruction will come on them suddenly, as labor pains on a pregnant woman, and they will not escape. (I Thessalonians 5:1-3)***
>
> ***Do you not know that the wicked will not inherit the kingdom of God? Do not be deceived:***

Neither the sexually immoral nor idolaters nor adulterers nor male prostitutes nor homosexual offenders nor thieves nor the greedy nor drunkards nor slanderers nor swindlers will inherit the kingdom of God. (I Corinthians 6:9-10)

BREAKDOWN OF LAW, ORDER

Those of you who are, or have been, behind bars can better visualize, perhaps, what the results of a complete breakdown of society would bring; and the resulting destruction that would ensue! You have perhaps felt the fear of being imprisoned with others, some with darkened and destitute minds; those who have only known a steady diet of hate, anger, lust and selfishness all their lives.

Imagine in your mind's eye, what would happen, if the inside guards were all removed to the outer walls for a time and all were left to do as they please. If just that amount of order, restraints and restrictions were taken away, then look out! Within the prison walls would be a microcosm (a small scale version) of all societies on the outside if present existing law and order would be completely broken down. Would you like to live or even try to exist in such a world where *all* RESTRAINTS were removed - both good and bad?

Let your mind imagine and envision the sequence of events that would unfold. How long do you think anything would last? How long do you think you would live? Your only chance of a day to day survival would be to become a murderous beast as part of a gang perhaps, and that would only be a fragile day by day existence until someone else outsmarted or double crossed you. We've had a few horrible situations where restraints have been removed within a prison confine and we know the gruesome story that soon unfolded. It became a literal untenable hell within a few hour's time! Yet individuals and groups of people in all countries of the world are trying their best to destroy existing law and order. They would like to destroy God and the blessings that He has produced by destroying the fruits of goodness.

Who would ever choose to spend an eternity where the law of *no restraint* would prevail? It would indeed be a literal Hell, regardless of any good sounding name painted on the gate. Who in their right mind would even elect to live on earth if total lawlessness, hate, selfishness, and all its resulting suffering prevailed? Lawlessness seems to flourish and *looks inviting,* only when operated in a society of moral restraints in which to hide. When lawlessness gains the upper hand and becomes the controlling factor, it soon *feeds* on *itself* and spirals to DESTRUCTION. This is the reason God cannot tolerate SIN in any form. LAWLESSNESS is *increasing* on earth! But because of certain restraints from God, which will in time be removed, it will take a few years to reach the fulfillment as spoken of in the Scripture. This time is indicated throughout the Bible as the LAST DAYS.

> ***"The great day of the Lord is near — near and coming quickly. Listen! The cry on the day of the Lord will be bitter, the shouting of the warrior there. That day will be a day of wrath, a day of distress and anguish, a day of trouble and ruin, a day of darkness and gloom, a day of clouds and blackness, a day of trumpet and battle cry against the fortified cities and against the corner towers. I will bring distress on the people and they will walk like blind men, be-***

cause they have sinned against the Lord. Their blood will be poured out like dust and their entrails like filth. Neither their silver nor their gold will be able to save them on the day of the Lord's wrath. In the fire of his jealousy the whole world will be consumed, for he will make a sudden end of all who live in the earth." (Zephaniah 1:14-18)

But you, brothers, are not in darkness so that this day should surprise you like a thief. You are all sons of the light and sons of the day. We do not belong to the night or to the darkness. So then, let us not be like others, who are asleep, but let us be alert and self-controlled. For those who sleep, sleep at night, and those who get drunk, get drunk at night. But since we belong to the day, let us be self-controlled, putting on faith and love as a breastplate, and the hope of salvation as a helmet. (I Thessalonians 5:4-8)

What a wise and loving God we have. He has established His Word and published decrees that point the way to happiness and peace. He strives constantly to penetrate our mind and conscience by every means possible with the truth that He *does exist*, and that His way is the *only* WAY for true life and happiness.

God is well aware that even the slightest deviation from His established way will create certain undesirable results. He is aware that those deviations in turn will cause ever greater degrading events which would finally result in total chaos, destruction, and the death of this planet. If He would allow this to happen, all His creation effort would go down the tube; the whole universe would be ultimately destroyed! His initial plan would thus be frustrated by one of His created beings, (a fallen archangel called Satan) since everything God created and purposed would then come to naught. Thus Satan would ultimately be the *winner!*

This is Satan's egotistical ploy. Even in his present defeated condition, he is trying to destroy as much as he can. He is not only a self appointed enemy of God, a traitor and a deceiver, but also an avid ENEMY of *man!* He will use you as a sacrificial tool to try to accomplish his own goal and then destroy you, without hesitation, showing no compassion or concern.

Satan cannot create the smallest atom or bring a photon of light in existence. He can only tear down and cause the destruction of that which God has created. Isn't this very close to the action of rampaging delinquents whose greatest acts are to damage or destroy what others have so lovingly and laboriously built? Yet, they themselves are totally incapable of designing or creating something useful.

The Future World With Christ

GOD IS IN CONTROL

Don't be misled, God is *not* in a last ditch stand in the waging of wars and skirmishes with a mastermind called Satan. *God is not* in a defensive situation! *On the contrary*, God, is still in *quiet control*, having already established the rules and the limits in which Satan and deluded mankind can operate. They will operate within this set arena, and the play acting will then come to a conclusion in God's own set time frame as already PRE-DETERMINED. The end date is already known by God and the outcome has been established and published.

Satan is still a created being of the angelic host, and I might add, also a *defeated* one; for Christ overcame him when He arose from the grave. Satan's time in heaven and on earth has *already been decreed!*

> ***And I saw an angel coming down out of heaven, having the key to the Abyss and holding in his hand a great chain. He seized the dragon, that ancient serpent, who is the devil, or Satan, and bound him for a thousand years. He threw him into the Abyss, and locked and sealed it over him, to keep him from deceiving the nations any more until the thousand years were ended. After that, he must be set free for a short time.***
> ***(Revelation 20:1-3)***

His binding judgment will come on the *exact day*

God has already set and proclaimed. God is not yet ready to pour out His wrath and redeem the earth as He promises He will in the "last day!" God is using Satan's influence and rampage on earth as a test arena to establish the character and free choice actions of all mankind. Our Christian character developed by free-choice of options cannot grow in a situation where no trials or tribulations are found.

> *"No one can serve two masters. Either he will hate the one and love the other, or he will be devoted to the one and despise the other. You cannot serve both God and Money. (Matthew 6:24)*
>
> *Blessed is the man who perseveres under trial, because when he has stood the test, he will receive the crown of life that God has promised to those who love him. (James 1:12)*

"If the Lord be God, follow Him: but if Baal, then follow him." (Ref. I Kings 18:21). The people of Elijah's day made a choice. We have to make the same decision of which god we are willing to serve, as every individual has had to do, since being placed on this earth.

Satan and the corrupt human race which he has misled have been allotted a specific time span to show all the universe that man's way under Satan's control can only lead to ultimate chaos and destruction. We won't need any investigative committee to tell us nor will anyone question God's Word after the test results are all in. All the created beings in the universe will have the answer! When the "day of the Lord" arrives then God will pour out His wrath on the remaining corrupt governments and nations of the world for a 3½ year period of time. "If those days were not cut short," we read, "then all human flesh would be destroyed."

> *For then there will be great distress, unequaled*

from the beginning of the world until now — and never to be equaled again. If those days had not been cut short, no one would survive, but for the sake of the elect those days will be shortened. (Matthew 24:21-22)

All nations will FALL! All human effort will be paralyzed and finally come *to naught*. But out of these ashes will rise a new age (a new world order); the beginning of God's Kingdom on earth which will last forever.

THE NEW AGE

Christ will come as KING OF KINGS and LORD OF LORDS of the whole earth and take charge of the new kingdom of God on earth. The saints, or born again ones, will help to rule and reign in God's Kingdom, first on earth, then undoubtedly in the universe.

Blessed and holy are those who have part in the first resurrection. The second death has no power over them, but they will be priests of God and of Christ and will reign with him for a thousand years. (Revelation 20:6)

Christ came the first time as a sacrifice for the sins of mankind and to preach (proclaim) the coming kingdom of God on earth.

The scroll of the prophet Isaiah was handed to him. Unrolling it, he found the place where it is written:

"The Spirit of the Lord is on me, because he has anointed me to preach good news to the poor. He has sent me to proclaim freedom for the prisoners and recovery of sight for the blind, to release the oppressed, to proclaim the year of the Lord's favor." (Luke 4:17-19)

The next time He comes will be as *King* and *Lord* to rule with a rod of iron. The earth will be redeemed from the curse of sin, that was imposed when man was tempted and fell. All outside evil forces will be removed. Peace, happiness, joy, freedom, plenty, love and righteousness will be the hallmark of this *new age*.

> ***Then the angel showed me the river of the water of life, as clear as crystal, flowing from the throne of God and of the Lamb down the middle of the great street of the city. On each side of the river stood the tree of life, bearing twelve crops of fruit, yielding its fruit every month. And the leaves of the tree are for the healing of the nations. No longer will there be any curse. The throne of God and of the Lamb will be in the city, and his servants will serve him. They will see his face, and his name will be on their foreheads. There will be no more night. They will not need the light of a lamp or the light of the sun, for the Lord God will give them light. And they will reign for ever and ever.***
> ***(Revelation 22:1-5)***

JUDGMENT TIME

Sin, as we know it today, will be dealt with severely and if necessary, by *capital punishment!* The people will be forceably taught and will obey the rules and laws of God that will bring all the attributes noted above to fulfillment. Christ and His saints "will rule the earth for a 1000 years with a rod of iron," but with great *love* and *concern*. (Rev. 2:26-27). The people will receive unheard of blessings! In this new age it will not be an option whether one will, or will not, obey. It will be *imperative*, until all learn for their own good! Even then many on earth will be misled by Satan when he is released for a short spell at the end of the 1000 year period. Many who have lived will still rebel and choose to follow evil, even though they have experienced and enjoyed the utopic blessings of Christ's Kingdom, for a millenium. Their names will be blotted out of the Lamb's Book of Life.

> ***Then death and Hades were thrown into the lake of fire. The lake of fire is the second death. If anyone's name was not found written in the book of life, he was thrown into the lake of fire. (Revelation 20:14-15)***

Satan after His release, for a short period of time, will test those born or raised up during that age. He will then be bound again, properly judged and sentenced, and will be cast into the lake of fire for all eternity.

> ***When the thousand years are over, Satan will be released from his prison and will go out to deceive the nations in the four corners of the earth — Gog and Magog — to gather them for battle. In number they are like the sand on the seashore. They marched across the breadth of the earth and surrounded the camp of God's people, the city he loves. But fire came down from heaven and devoured them. And the devil, who deceived them, was thrown into the lake of burning sulfur, where the beast and the false prophet had been thrown. They will be tormented day and night for ever and ever. (Revelation 20:7-10)***

You'd better believe Satan's days are exactly numbered by God. HE IS A LOST CAUSE! So why let him still gather you up as fuel for his fire? It has been said that "misery loves company," but I personally don't care for his misery or his company for all eternity in the LAKE OF FIRE.

Just remember you are the No. 1 actor on the world stage at this present time! It depends from which source you take your cues that determines *your part* in the next act of the world drama. If from God and Jesus Christ, then you will be given an opportunity to continue to perform on the universal stage for all eternity; but if from Satan, you will be swept out to eternal destruction with him and his fallen angels.

When the curtain comes crashing down on the present stage, the lights will go out and judgment time will begin. This could be in a few short years, or decades, if talking about mankind as a whole, or a much shorter time span, for you and me individually, if death should intervene before that time.

THE LAST ENEMY - DEATH

God has had to decree the death penalty for sinning. This was done in order that sin would not become an eternal state in the universe. When God made man he made him a physical being of earthly material (dirt). Death came upon mankind as a result of Adam's sin and so, "to dust shall we all return." Mankind was thus only allowed physical life until God determines, by individual actions, who really desires to obey His commands and will. Those who obey will be resurrected and given a new, eternal, celestial body. Those who disobey are eventually cast into the lake of fire. At the end of time, however, even death will be destroyed by Christ as mankind is finally brought into harmony with God's will.

> ***Then the end will come, when he hands over the kingdom to God the Father after he has de-***

stroyed all dominion, authority and power. For he must reign until he has put all his enemies under his feet. The last enemy to be destroyed is death. (I Corinthians 15:24-26)

God uses death for much the same reason as we perhaps utilize an oil filter on a car engine. We use a filter to clean out all the harmful foreign particles in the oil that could eventually destruct the engine or cause its malfunction. Our new expensive product is thus faithfully protected from destruction. God has established all the rules, since He's setting the standard by which we operate as His creation. He has had to remind us again and again that the payoff of the game we play is this: "The wages (or earnings) for SIN is death." First the physical death of our body then later the second *death* (spiritual death) which will last for all eternity. Physical death awaits every man, woman, boy, girl or child born on earth. "Flesh and blood (and sin) cannot and *shall not* inherit the kingdom of God" - declares a *righteous* and *holy* God.

This requires two important transformations, if we are going to be part of God's eternity. We are going to have to get that payment or penalty for sin that we have earned, transferred to someone else (since we've all earned it) and we will have to find ourselves a new jump suit to live in! It's obvious that decayed dirt and dust will not make for a suitable universal space suit. It took specialists about 10 years of research and twenty million dollars to create one of their own design that recently lasted an hour in outer space.

I declare to you, brothers, that flesh and blood cannot inherit the kingdom of God, nor does the perishable inherit the imperishable. (I Corinthians 15:50)

A NEW BODY

Our heavenly suit will have to house our *spirit life* in a new *celestial body* that can withstand the rigors of universal space travel. It will have to last for all eternity. It will have to be INDESTRUCTIBLE! It cannot be of physical or earthly materials that can get hurt, bent, broken or destroyed as easily as it does now. It will have to operate in all physical environments be it extremes of heat, cold, humidity, dryness, vacuum or pressure. The only person in all the universe capable of doing that refitting job for us is God's son, the Lord Jesus Christ - who created all things.

> ***If there is a natural body, there is also a spiritual body. So it is written: "The first man Adam became a living being", the last Adam, a life-giving spirit. The spiritual did not come first, but the natural, and after that the spiritual. The first man was of the dust of the earth, the second man from heaven. As was the earthly man, so are those who are of the earth; and as is the man from heaven, so also are those who are of heaven. And just as we have borne the likeness of the earthly man, so shall we bear the likeness of the man from heaven. (I Corinthians 15:45-49)***

Even Christ died on earth in his physical body, not because of His own sins, for He had none, but for yours and mine. Since He was free from sin, (he never once gave allegiance to Satan in any form), God could raise Him from the dead, and give Him a new spiritual, celestial body good for all the ages of time. And that body can space travel anywhere in the universe in an instant of time at the speed of thought.

Christ in his *new glorified* BODY now sits at the right hand of God our Father as our HIGH PRIEST and MEDIATOR. The pull of gravity, the boundaries of time and the tears and sorrows brought on by sin will all be removed from us when we obtain these newly created bodies. We will shout with joy at our new found freedoms and the praise of God the Father will flow from our lips forevermore as we are transformed or resurrected into this new celestial form.

> ***Shout for joy to the Lord, all the earth. Serve the Lord with gladness; come before him with joyful songs. Know that the Lord is God. It is he who made us, and we are his; we are his people, the sheep of his pasture. (Psalms 100:1-3)***

Anyone who believes God's Word and accepts Christ as their Lord and Savior and who has the Spirit of Christ living within, will be raised up at the *resurrection* or *rapture* by Christ. They will receive eternal life, as a *separate entity*, by receiving this new body. This is the transfer point, the jump suit changeover for all Christians.

> ***For the Lord himself will come down from heaven, with a loud command, with the voice of the archangel and with the trumpet call of God, and the dead in Christ will rise first. After that, we who are still alive and are left will be caught up with them in the clouds to meet the Lord in the air. And so we will be with the Lord forever. (I Thessalonians 4:16-17)***

MUCK, MELONS OR MORONS

In our delusions we have sunk to the lowest levels of

intelligence. We have by self education, by our limited knowledge, come to believe Satan's great lie; that all things in the universe just happened, or came into being by chance, by a flip of the cosmic dice. The last thing he would ever acknowledge is God as Creator. He would have us believe that this beautiful and unique world of ours, which is only one perhaps of 10 billion very similar worlds created by God, in just our galaxy alone, that somehow it just found itself existing; idly standing by waiting for the proclaimed evolutionary cycle of life to begin. By chance it was rotating exactly at the right distance and times around a small lonely star, so that it could support the 3 billion life forms in the complex matrix which have been found and identified today.

What murky morass we tread as we allow our educators (the supposed intelligensia of our day) to teach our children that we are nothing more than an amoeba, a vegetable, a dumb furry mammal made smart by *self-education.* The more degrees and doctorates cranked out by secular universities the lower the SAT scores become in our schools. Man's best education standards, without the wisdom and inputs from God, will lead only to guesses and folly. Only Satan with all his cunning and deceit, could pull off such a coup as evolution on a gullible and unsuspecting human race. We read in Scriptures, "God made this world and He made it to be inhabited."

> ***For this is what the Lord says — he who created the heavens, he is God; he who fashioned and made the earth, he founded it; he did not create it to be empty but formed it to be inhabited — (Isaiah 45:18)***

He created man and placed him here to rule the earth. But, instead, we have plundered, burned, cut and destroyed, killed and eliminated about everything left under our control. The continued existence of any life on earth is in grave *danger*. Thanks be to God. He has promised that before man destroys the earth and himself, He will cut that time short. Thank God for His repeated promise to redeem both mankind and the earth from the curse of sin.

> ***We know that the whole creation has been groaning as in the pains of childbirth right up to the present time. Not only so, but we ourselves, who have the firstfruits of the Spirit, groan inwardly as we wait eagerly for our adoption as sons, the redemption of our bodies. (Romans 8:22-23)***
>
> ***And they sang a new song: "You are worthy to take the scroll and to open its seals, because you were slain, and with your blood you purchased men for God from every tribe and language and people and nation. You have made them to be a kingdom and priests to serve our God, and they will reign on the earth." (Revelation 5:9-10)***

Without this promise, future hope or happiness in this life, would be dismal and dim indeed. Man has not evolved from a morass of protoplasm to the great visionary scientist of wisdom and understanding that he would like to claim. But he has fallen from the heights to the depths of confusion and despair. In order to have the necessary time spans in which to bring about the concept of evolutionary changes as required and suggested, this grandiose *hatching scheme* would require millions and billions of years of minute, almost non-existent, development and change. Imagine, if you can, the scenario of change from muck to molasses to modern morons, in 16 billion unnoticed steps. No such changes have ever been proven or shown by history or archeological evidence to be true for the 3 billion final species now on earth!

All specimens are in their FINAL FORM and there has been *no evidences* or *proof* of any such change since their creation. A missing link? Under such a plan there should be 10 BILLIONS of missing links around somewhere for each of the 3 billion final life forms on earth. Don't look for just *one* but let us expand our scope as there are at least three hundred thousand billion out there if evolution be true. With all the billions of years supposedly required to produce our present body form, it only lasts for a few years, and then decays and goes back to dust exactly as God has revealed in His Word.

> ***The length of our days is seventy years — or eighty, if we have the strength; yet their span is but trouble and sorrow, for they quickly pass, and we fly away. (Psalms 90:10)***

And all this happens amid tears, sorrow, sickness, pain and suffering. That doesn't sound like too great an end design, considering all the preliminaries and the eons of time supposedly required for its manufacture, as claimed by those who disbelieve God's Word regarding creation. God has promised, however, to all who believe and accept His way, a *new celestial body* that will be good for all the ages of time. And this we will get in an INSTANT of time at the last trumpet call.

> ***Listen, I tell you a mystery: We will not all sleep, but we will all be changed — in a flash, in the twinkling of an eye, at the last trumpet. For the trumpet will sound, the dead will be raised imperishable, and we will be changed.***

(I Corinthians 15:51-52)

I can never understand how a professing Christian can really look forward to receiving this new body promised by God in an *instant* of time, (in the twinkling of an eye) and at the same time accept the theory that the temporary and temporal one they now have required millions and billions of years of time to come into being in its present form. I doubt that anyone can truly believe both statements AS FACT at the same time.

Wrong Ways Made Right

RELIGIOUS BUT LOST

Again, in summary, in regard to spiritual matters and the keeping of the laws of God, who can be saved? *All people* if they so choose! Who can be saved by their *own* efforts? The resounding answer is NO ONE! Without a reconnection to God all our so-called contrived righteousness is as filthy rags. No one can ever *become worthy* of being saved by his own self efforts, by being good, or religious, or by keeping the law or any part of it. The majority of the people of the world *do not believe God's* Word on this subject.

This world is teeming with all types of people and *most* are *very religious*. It has been my privilege in the last few years to travel into many different countries on mission and other work, and I can testify that the human

race is indeed a bunch of *religious nuts*, whether in America, Africa, Asia or the islands of the sea. Everywhere I go I find people chanting, jumping, swaying, rolling around, building idols, cutting flesh, sitting for hours like statues or repetitiously performing some type of formal ceremony. They clang gongs and cymbals, make music or beat drums, just because they have intuitive knowledge from the universe around them that there is someone greater than they - and they are all trying to *find favor* with that god of *unknown* gods. All generations of peoples, of all ages on earth, have been *religious*.

I know of certain people here in America that go from one religious musical concert to another and they think they are being very religious. And in a true meaning of the word, they are. But being religious will not ensure eternal life no matter how sincere, how old the system, how good it feels, or how much pomp or ceremony is involved. This, according to the Word of Jesus Christ, is the broad way that many follow, as they march to their own destruction.

> ***Enter through the narrow gate. For wide is the gate and broad is the road that leads to destruction, and many enter through it. But small is the gate and narrow the road that leads to life, and only a few find it.***
> ***"Watch out for false prophets. They come to you in sheep's clothing, but inwardly they are ferocious wolves. By their fruit you will recognize them. Do people pick grapes from thornbushes, or figs from thistles?***
> ***"Not everone who says to me, 'Lord, Lord,' will enter the kingdom of heaven, but only he who does the will of my Father who is in heaven. Many will say to me on that day, 'Lord, Lord, did we not prophesy in your name, and in your name drive out demons and perform many miracles? Then I will tell them plainly, 'I never knew you. Away from me, you evildoers!'***
> ***(Matthew 7:13-16, 21-23)***

ALL OR NOTHING

The point that should be made is this: All the basic facts concerning right versus wrong, evil versus good, death versus life has come by a revelation from God. This has been revealed to us by three or four methods. First; by the written inspired Word of God, the Holy Scriptures. Next; by our observation and witness of the orderly universe which surrounds us. Always; by our inner conscience. And last, but not least; by the actual appearing of Jesus Christ the "Living Word" in this world.

If God's revelations are false, being a delusion and a dream of our own making and not from God, then that dream would be a false standard to follow. It would follow that there would be NO standard (law) at all for man. If that be so, then any of man's ideas or thoughts, regardless of being weird or normal, rational or illogical, right or wrong, would be as good as another. Wrong could mean right, evil could mean good, and death could mean life, or so it would be imagined! Many are trying to live under these very conditions. Remember Satan's lying whispers into the ears of Adam and Eve in the Garden of Eden. "You can be like gods. You shall *not* surely die!" But die they did - and all their progeny after them to this very day!

On the other hand if God's revelation is true then we had better heed that word; yes, and ALL of that Word. Specifically as professing Christians if we apprehend God's spirit and in our mind believe God's revelation about Himself, then it behooves us to continue to obey that Word in *all it's detail*. We do not have the option to pick and choose only those goodies that somehow are more palatable and acceptable to our lower nature and conveniently ignore the rest of His revelation. If we think about it, it becomes obvious; it is either *all or none*. God's Word is either ALL TRUE or it's ALL FALSE! If we are going to rewrite for our own benefit, it doesn't leave Him with much authority - or us *with much hope*.

I know of teachers and pastors in some major denominations who preach and teach a very fundamental salvation message - for which I praise God! But seemingly the total Bible message for them is centered in a very few verses of the book of Acts or the other gospels where, historically, the start of the church is described. The other sixty some attached books of the Bible either have little meaning to them or else they are not considered relevant. This should not be!

In fact some may be so bold as to discount, and even discredit others who study and proclaim the other 90% of Scripture. They, somehow, overlook the fact that Revelation is the only book in all the Scriptures that God has promised a special blessing for just reading or hearing its words.

Their attitude shows not only a lack of Biblical knowledge and a shortness of Spiritual wisdom regarding the Bible as the total Word of God, but it also shows their proneness to accept Satans dialogue, which far too often, presents an incomplete or 'crippled' gospel message. A message that often justifies the present religious situation of membership, divisions, suspicions, and tradition that weaken and divide the true body of Christ, the church.

When Christ came to earth He came proclaiming the *coming* KINGDOM of GOD! Should we as followers do otherwise? An undue emphasis on the historical acts of Christ at one specific point in time 2000 years ago is *not* the *total* gospel message that should be proclaimed to the exclusion of all else.

Christ was with the Father before the world was created. We read He created the earth and the universe. It was Christ who walked and talked with Adam and Eve and the Old Testament patriarchs before the church age. It was indeed Christ who was born into the human race as the physical manifestation of God; who lived and taught among men and laid down His life as a complete sacrifice for the sins of mankind. It is this same Christ who now sits on the right hand of the throne of God as our High Priest and mediator. It will be the same Christ who shall return again and who will establish the Kingdom of God upon earth. He shall be "King of Kings and Lord of Lords" over the whole earth during this coming 1000 years of peace. Christ is Creator and Redeemer, the great HIGH PRIEST and future King.

It is the same Christ who shall resurrect from the grave all persons who have experienced a new spiritual rebirth and will translate (or change) all of like spirit who are still alive at that time.

This is the overall story that the Bible reveals - the COMPLETE gospel message!

It includes the restoration of the earth from the devastating result of sin. It includes the redemption of our spirit as well as the deliverance of our body from death. It will encompass the total rehabilitation of the plant and animal kingdom, ravaged by the powerful and degrading effects of the curse of original sin.

Included in this great message is the account of Christ's first advent but also included is His promised 'soon return'. In reviewing such precious teachings as the 'new birth' and 'baptism' we find they are only mentioned perhaps fifty or sixty times in Scripture. Now this does not in any way detract or minimize their importance - for *all scripture* is important even if mentioned only once! But what of Christs' second coming? Shall we ignore it and treat it as being unimportant? Especially since it is referred to, not a few score times, but over 2500 times in some form throughout the Bible. Someone has said that every fifteenth word in the New Testament refers to the second advent. It should be the one event that is the only true hope of all Christians. For only at Christ's coming is it promised that Christians will be resurrected from the grave, or translated if still living and will be given a new celestial body. If you are a Christian and *not* looking forward to this great event, what in all the world (or universe) are you looking for?

It is not enough to know *about* Christ - just about what He did in a historical sense 2000 years ago while on earth during His short stay - and then to repeat this over and over in endless detail. In our Sunday Schools we teach our children endless stories about various patriarchs, prophets, and kings but never once tie the whole message of the Bible together or discuss its importance to the overall Kingdom of God. Let us move on as the Word admonishes; from the "milk" of babes to the more "solid food" of mature Christians! (Ref. Hebrews 5:12-14)

We not only need to know Christ historically but we must know Him intimately NOW, to experience His forgiving *power* in our lives and to do His will. We must believe, acknowledge and present His claims and *promises* for the future as well, as these will not only change our lives - but the lives of others around us. The Kingdom of God includes and incorporates all these elements of the past, present and future. Christ is ETERNAL!

We are on dangerous ground when we pick and choose, believe and proclaim, only those portions of Gods Holy Word that catches our fancy. Undue emphasis by some is being placed on some specific gift of the Spirit, on tongues, on the second coming, on the first advent, on prophetic events, or angels, or the historical acts of Christ. A distorted or crippled gospel is one that may be correct in itself as far as it goes, but completely out of balance (or emphasis) with other basic truths of the Bible. Like a finely designed instrument each part of the Bible is in complete harmony with all others and each enhances the whole.

Let us be careful to treat all great doctrines with equal consideration, keeping a balanced perspective of each one as it fits into the whole of Scripture. Satan can, and many times does, lead us astray (or to the extreme) in many areas of our physical life - and he will do the same thing if we permit him in our Spiritual talk and walk.

Once we have taken steps to acknowledge that God *is* and pay heed to His Word, we'd better continue to inquire and to grow in the knowledge of His way. A quasi belief that many have, that God merely exists, is probably worse than NO BELIEF at all. You may start out in the beginning with a few doubts which would be normal in a learning situation, but it will be disastrous if you end up that same way. All the demons in Hell and on earth and even Satan himself believes God's revelation about himself more emotionally and fervently than that. THEY TREMBLE!

> ***But someone will say, "You have faith; I have deeds."***
> ***Show me your faith without deeds, and I will show you my faith by what I do. You believe that there is one God. Good! Even the demons believe that - and shudder. (James 2:18-19)***

There is only one way, *only one path*; and God has already provided it. There is only *one mediator* between God and man and that is the man, THE LORD JESUS CHRIST. All others who try to climb into the sheep fold by some other way are imposters and will be cast out.

> ***"I tell you the truth, the man who does not enter the sheep pen by the gate, but climbs in by some other way, is a thief and a robber. The man who enters by the gate is the shepherd of his sheep.***
> ***Therefore Jesus said again, "I tell you the truth, I am the gate for the sheep. All who ever came before me were thieves and robbers, but the***

sheep did not listen to them. I am the gate; whoever enters through me will be saved. He will come in and go out, and find pasture.
(John 10:1-2,7-9)

God quite frankly is fed up with our good intentions, our man-made traditions and our "Reader's Digest" version of His righteousness. We're mostly ignorant of God's way, we're misled and a large majority of the populace is out of control heading for the dump heap. Outside of that I guess everything else is OK with mankind. The weather is fine, at least for today.

ALL ARE JUDGED

From the eternal spiritual point of view it really doesn't matter who you are, if you are *imprisoned* physically or to a life of sin and slavery, or both. It doesn't matter if you are a highly paid executive for a major corporation, or a social worker or a law enforcement official, or if you are a farmer or a merchant or a housewife or a young business person. The fact of the matter, the plain truth is that if you DO NOT have Christ abiding within as your savior, you are just plain 'LOST' - and that for all eternity.

Rather, we have renounced secret and shameful ways; we do not use deception, nor do we distort the word of God. On the contrary, by setting forth the truth plainly we commend ourselves to every man's conscience in the sight of God. And even if our gospel is veiled, it is veiled to those who are perishing. The god of this age has blinded the minds of unbelievers, so that they cannot see the light of the gospel of the glory of Christ, who is the image of God.

(II Corinthians 4:2-4)

And this is the testimony: God has given us eternal life, and this life is in his Son. He who has the Son has life; he who does not have the Son of God does not have life. (I John 5:11,12)

On our own merits, without Christ's saving power, we are condemned to die the second death. We have all broken some part or all of God's moral law and are part of the Adamic race so the first death is automatic. But the second one is by our own *choosing!*

In your present condition you may have a short or long record sheet on file or no record at all. You may regularly go to a church or spend your time in a bar. You and I, on our own, are not worthy, in God's sight and His righteousness, to receive eternal life; and as a consequence you and I will die for our sins. That is, unless we have found or will find a *substitute*; someone willing to take the death penalty for us! Wouldn't that be something to find someone who would volunteer to take our place behind bars if we were indeed incarcerated? Someone who would serve the remaining years on our sentence.

FIND A SCAPEGOAT

To find a scapegoat, someone willing to go on death row, to eat that last supper and take that last walk for us, would be about the ultimate for the human mind to fathom.

This is exactly what God has done for the human race, which stands justly judged and condemned. God has done this for the creation that has been found so wanting, fallen so short of His righteousness; that it can't be accepted in its present sinful condition.

God in the form of Jesus Christ (God's Son) came, was born into this world and *died willingly* on Calvary's cross, to shed His precious blood for your sins and mine, and for the sins of all mankind. He died as our substitute, thus paying the penalty for *our* sins.

> ***In fact, the law requires that nearly everything be cleansed with blood, and without the shedding of blood there is no forgiveness.***
>
> ***It was necessary, then, for the copies of the heavenly things to be purified with these sacrifices, but the heavenly things themselves with better sacrifices than these. For Christ did not enter a man-made sanctuary that was only a copy of the true one; he entered heaven itself, now to appear for us in God's presence. Nor did he enter heaven to offer himself again and again, the way the high priest enters the Most Holy Place every year with blood that is not his own. Then Christ would have had to suffer many times since the creation of the world. But now he has appeared once for all at the end of the ages to do away with sin by the sacrifice of himself. Just as man is destined to die once, and after that to face judgement, so Christ was sacrificed once to take away the sins of many people; and he will appear a second time, not to bear sin, but to bring salvation to those who are waiting for him. (Hebrews 9:22-28)***

No one knows why the shedding of blood is required for remission of sins and is satisfying in God's sight, but it is sufficient for Him even though we might not comprehend God's thoughts. God, in looking on the human race, finds that it is *totally bankrupt*, but, He in His grace and mercy looked down on the world in love and compassion. Salvation is totally by *God's Grace*, not man's effort. THERE IS NO OTHER WAY to be saved. We can build our idols, shave our heads, beat our drums, cut ourselves, fast and feast, meditate and wear peculiar garb, or go to formal ceremonies every day of the week or until the cows come home, but it will be to *no avail* . Our condemning sins will still be there and our separation from God will still exist because of our sins. God, in love, has already prepared the way and *paid* the *penalty* for YOUR SINS and mine. It is our privilege and *gain to accept* or it will be our *loss to reject* this gift so freely offered.

> ***For the message of the cross is foolishness to those who are perishing, but to us who are being saved it is the power of God. For it is written:***
> ***"I will destroy the wisdom of the wise; the intelligence of the intelligent I will frustrate."***
> ***(I Corinthians 1:18,19)***

If we are ever to live beyond this present life, we must recognize our sinful nature, the magnitude of our transgression against God's way; we must become aware of our *present condition.* This condition, if left unattended, will result in us receiving the full payment for sin, the second death.

ATONEMENT OF CHRIST

Our salvation and hope comes first by recognizing and turning from our sinful selfish ways and then accepting Jesus, God's son as our savior. When we acknowledge our lost condition, our unworthiness before God, and ask Jesus, (in Spirit), to come into our heart and life; the Holy righteousness of Christ, then, becomes our righteousness. This is the *atonement*!

We are then *hid* in Christ! When we, thus are in

Christ, as God looks upon us He does not see our unrighteousness, (the man-proposed righteousness which He cannot accept or tolerate), but He sees the *perfect righteousness* of Christ instead. Although we are still prone to failures and have guilt and sin in our lives, God sees only the attributes of Christ, which is blamelessness, perfection, and holiness. This is the SUBSTITUTING ATONEMENT, the present work of the resurrected Christ, who died for our sins that we might be justified before God.

> ***Since we have now been justified by his blood, how much more shall we be saved from God's wrath through him! For if, when we were God's enemies, we were reconciled to him through the death of his Son, how much more, having been reconciled, shall we be saved through his life! Not only is this so, but we also rejoice in God through our Lord Jesus Christ, through whom we have now received reconciliation.***
> ***(Romans 5:9-11)***

At the fall of man in the Garden of Eden, as we have noted, the spirit of God *departed* or was kept from man. Man was left a physical shell with his own choice of what was good or evil, and without the mind of Christ to guide him in right paths. He thus became a tool and pawn of Satan. In this condition a time limit was placed on his stay here on earth by an event that we now know as death.

WHAT IS SALVATION?

Man was thus left on his own with inputs from the evil spirit, (not the Holy Spirit) as he was devoid of God's guidance. The true life line had been severed by his *independent* action and sin.

This process is *reversed at salvation.* When man BELIEVES in Christ's death and resurrection, REPENTS of his sins, ACCEPTS His sacrifice for those sins, and follows Christ in the first act of obedience, baptism, the Holy Spirit is again restored to man. He is again plugged in to the POWER SOURCE. The actual presence of Christ in the spiritual realm, *lives within* the individual. We thus become the receptacle or temple of the Holy Ghost. And then can be guided into right choices and decisions. God says, "Know ye not that your body is the temple of the Holy Ghost?" (Ref.I Corinth. 6:19)

TWO NEW COMMANDMENTS

As Jesus was preaching, He stated that He was indeed *fulfilling* all of the law of the prophets. When asked, by those who were trying to ridicule Him, which of the ten commandments was most important to keep, He said "I'll sum them all up giving you two new commandments."

> ***Jesus replied: "Love the Lord your God with all your heart and with all your soul and with all your mind. This is the first and greatest commandment. And the second is like it: 'Love your neighbor as yourself'. All the Law and the Prophets hang on these two commandments." (Matthew 22:37-40)***

Now this does not mean that the original code has been done away with and we can now, as new followers, run out and break the commandments of God with impunity. No, it just means that instead of us nibbling away at the commandments from the outside, trying to keep a few to try to find favor with God, we now have the actual source of eternal life within us. Jesus wants to come and abide within us to live His life in us, and thus it will be reflected from inside to outside.

The basis of this new *life* is LOVE. "God is love," a simple statement, which we don't fully comprehend! Love always *outflows* in goodness or good will *to others*. (Ref. I John 4:8). Thus with Christ within and His love being reflected through us to others, we can now begin to keep all the old commandments (law) in a totally new way - "IN SPIRIT AND TRUTH". For example, one of the original commandments states "Thou shall not commit adultery." That is actual sexual intercourse outside of your marriage partner. Think of all the ramifications, the heartaches, hatred, tears, suffering, pain, killings, diseases, etc. that have been caused as a result of breaking this one law. But Jesus said, "Whosoever looketh upon a woman to *lust* after her has committed *adultery* with her already in his heart - and whosoever hateth his brother is a *murderer*." (Ref. Matthew 5:28, I John 3:15)

Does this sound like the gates have been thrown open and we can do as we please? That the law can now be ignored? Just the opposite! From this we can see we have already sinned when the thought is allowed to play upon the emotions and not necessarily just at the point that we might find opportunity to commit the so-called physical act. Thus you see what is needed is not just elimination of a few selected physical acts but for our whole ungodly act to be cleaned *inside* by new management. We must come under new leadership, our whole *attitude* must be *changed*. We must receive new direction, new motivation; outside help for INSIDE CHANGE.

There is no such thing as tweaking or shaping up the

old charactor or the reshaping or changing of some of its parts to make it acceptable to God. A new paint job won't make a sale to God, even if it's *antique* WHITE. It is too far gone! It can't be refurbished! It takes a *new* BIRTH, a *new* CREATION! Christ comes and lives within, when invited, and it is HIS LIFE and SPIRIT that takes over our motivation and outreach, through the sequence of our mind, brain and body. Paul admonishes us in Philippians 2:2, to "be like minded" ... "being of one accord" in Christ. Thus we become one in spirit and purpose! The only life that can be pleasing to God is the one that comes from *Him* who redeemed us. We are admonished as Christians not to *grieve* the Holy Spirit by allowing self to regain control of our will, but to be very sensitive to His guidance and presence within.

> ***And do not grieve the Holy Spirit of God, with whom you were sealed for the day of redemption. Get rid of all bitterness, rage and anger, brawling and slander, along with every form of malice. Be kind and compassionate to one another, forgiving each other, just as in Christ God forgave you. (Ephesians 4:30-32)***

CHRISTIAN GROWTH CYCLE

In our Christian growth it is only after the more obvious sins are identified and eliminated that we will begin to discover the ever present multitude of more devious sins we previously had not suspected. The remaining years of our lives as Christians, if successful, will be spent in developing the character and habits that are pleasing to God. Character and attributes that will be used for an eternity must be developed in life's training school. And this *only* by the working of the Spirit and the MIND of Christ within us. It is a process that will continue for the rest of our earthly existence. We must understand this process and nature of Christian growth as God works in our lives, day by day, by His Spirit, to bring us to the knowledge and wisdom of His ways.

Some years ago my wife and I purchased a citrus ranch in southern California where we raised oranges, lemons and avocados. Prior to our purchase the previous owner had to disk around and under the trees on a monthly basis to keep the ever growing weeds under control. This disking operation destroyed the low hanging limbs of the orange tree, hurting production, destroyed many of the roots and necessitated making new furrows for the bi-monthly irrigations. We immediately went to a new system called *noncultivation.* The ground was carefully cultivated and the furrows for irrigation were put in. From that time on, the ground was never cultivated or disturbed for the remaining years that we owned the property. This necessitated, in the beginning, the spraying and killing of the weeds every week or so with a toxic oil spray. The object was never to let *one weed*, ever, go to seed. We would literally grow all the weed seeds out of the ground over the next few years.

At the start of the program the healthy weeds would grow three feet high in a few weeks, before they began to set forth seed pods. We would faithfully spray and kill all of them before that time. As months went on we soon discovered to our dismay, some weeds that were only a foot high were beginning to set seed pods. As more time went on we were soon spraying weeds which were only six inches in height as they, believe it or not, were actually going to seed. It began to dawn on us that we had a *serious* PROBLEM. We had on our hands, a whole field full of weeds, that were so smart they were somehow beginning to out-think us. By then I had noticed some weeds coming through the ground less than an inch high with seed pods attached! Could it be true? Do weeds think? Were these really thinking and trying to outsmart us by cunning and devious means?

One fair day as we contemplated on this somewhat startling development, the truth finally dawned on our clouded intelligence. The smaller weeds, with their quicker cycle of seed reproduction, had been there all the time hidden among the taller more lush weeds - merrily going to seed! These smaller ones were happily growing and reproducing while we were watching and fighting the larger ones with their longer cycle time of reproduction. It was only as the large ones were eliminated and taken completely out of the picture that we were finally able to detect and observe the smaller weeds that previously had escaped our attention. They had been recycling in joyous fruition all the time and we were not aware of their presence!

FINE TUNE

This is a realistic example of the sins within our own lives. As we become Christians we are obviously aware of those major events in our lives that kept us from communing with God.

Maybe as born again Christians, we think that by eliminating a few big obvious clankers, maybe by physical restraint, New Year's resolutions, or other drastic measures, we can instantly, become good disciples (100% Christians) and pleasing to God without any maintenance. But not so! Most of these sins we could count on one hand. Sure, God has provided atonement for our sins through Jesus Christ, but we must take up our cross daily. Our total life, from the moment of this great decision, must be centered in the development of Christ-like character within. We will soon find even after we have received His Spirit it will take God's help, through painful trial and error, to eliminate all those 'little foxes' that previously had escaped our attention. Only by our abiding in the Word of God and by having the oil (a type of the Holy Spirit) applied in profuse amounts in our lives will the total population of weeds (our waywardness) be destroyed. This guarantees our acceptability as true *disciples.*

> ***Therefore, since we are surrounded by such great cloud of witnesses, let us throw off everything that hinders and the sin that so easily entangles, and let us run with perseverance the race marked out for us. Let us fix our eyes on Jesus, the author and perfecter of our faith, who for the joy set before him endured the cross, scorning its shame, and sat down at the right hand of the throne of God. Consider him who endured such opposition from sinful men so that you will not grow weary and lose heart.***
> ***(Hebrews 12:1-3)***

Only the spirit of Christ can accomplish this in our life after the new birth. It may take a lifetime to finally develop the mind and character of Christ within so that we can truly be used and led of God. What futility for us to sit rigidly in our little selected pews, ignoring the daily application of God's Word as the guide for our life. Many have never changed *one iota* in thought or deed from the time they first walked down the aisle to accept a new walk and a new way of life. What can these misled souls expect? Surely not a welcome with the words, "Well done, thou good and faithful servant!" - but a "*depart* from me you workers of iniquity. And there will be wailing and gnashing of teeth!"

They claim to know God, but by their actions they deny him. They are detestable, disobedient and unfit for doing anything good. (Titus 1:16)
But the subjects of the kingdom will be thrown outside, into the darkness, where there will be weeping and gnashing of teeth." (Matthew 8:12)

If we are serious about our Christian walk after eliminating the larger, obvious, and unacceptable sins from our life, we will begin to fine tune our character. Christ will reveal to us those petty, previously hidden, bad characteristics (those sins) that are just as *deadly* perhaps as the large obvious ones. The sins of jealousy, pride, lust, selfishness and anger will finally be exposed for all the ungodliness they represent in our lives.

Therefore, brothers, we have an obligation - but it is not to the sinful nature, to live according to it. For if you live according to the sinful nature, you will die; but if by the Spirit you put to death the misdeeds of the body, you will live, because those who are led by the Spirit of God are sons of God. (Romans 8:12-14)
Therefore each of you must put off falsehood and speak truthfully to his neighbor, for we are all members of one body. "In your anger do not sin." Do not let the sun go down while you are still angry, and do not give the devil a foothold. He who has been stealing must steal no longer, but must work, doing something useful with his own hands, that he may have something to share with those in need.
Do not let any unwholesome talk come out of your mouths, but only what is helpful for building others up according to their needs, that it may benefit those who listen. (Ephesians 4:25-29)

It's a paradox but as we grow in our Christian life we

will find those sins, which seemed so relatively *unimportant* in the beginning, are soon seen to be the basic ones at the root cause of all our problems! This is because the basic sin of mankind (self and selfishness) will be manifest in many and varied forms. To be sure the basic sin of Satan was SELF and SELFISHNESS and this also has to be the basic sin of man. With Christ's help, motivated by the Holy Word and guided by *the Holy Spirit*, victory can be found. Satan can be cast completely out of our lives! And we can finally reach that plateau of living that is pleasing in God's sight. The way will not be easy nor instantaneous. We must learn how to bind and rebuke Satan and bring all our waywardness and disobedience to Christ for a daily cleansing.

> ***If we claim to be without sin, we deceive ourselves and the truth is not in us. If we confess our sins, he is faithful and just and will forgive us our sins and purify us from all unrighteousness. (I John 1:8-9)***

LOVE OF GOD

If we do not grieve the Holy Spirit, if we walk in obedience to the Word and in the light of Christ's guidance, God's love will be reflected, through us, back TO GOD in true worship; and TO OTHERS (our neighbors) around us. Our outward actions will thus *agree* with the change within. They will then show the result of the change that has taken place. We will not try to use actions to affect a change. An apple tree bears fruit (apples) because in its heart it is an apple tree. No tree ever tries to bear apples just in order *to become* an apple tree. The outward fruit produced is always consistent with the inner being. One can never change the cause by *fiddling* with *effects*.

There are two basic philosophies of life in the world today. For those outside of Christ, the first is one of *getting*, of receiving, of *using others* for advantage and selfish gain. This is *inflow*, or SELFISHNESS! The second is concern for others, or *outflow*. Since love always outflows to others, love must have a recipient or expression or it turns within and becomes self love or selfishness.

When we are concerned for the well being of others above even our own self interests, that is true LOVE. The self love that inflows is CARNAL, the expressed love that outflows to others is *spiritual*. One is natural, the other is *supernatural*! The carnal, we receive at natural birth, the last we can only receive at the *new birth*. God's love is a *covenant love* - always out-flowing to us regardless of our attitude toward Him. He always wants the best for us. God's covenant love reflected through us will always be out-flowing to others - regardless of their attitude toward us.

This is REAL LOVE.

> ***Whoever does not love does not know God, because God is love. This is how God showed his love among us: He sent his one and only Son into the world that we might live through him. This is love: not that we loved God, but that he loved us and sent his Son as an atoning sacrifice for our sins.***
>
> ***We love because he first loved us. If anyone says, "I love God," yet hates his brother, he is a liar. For anyone who does not love his brother, whom he has seen, cannot love God, whom he has not seen. And he has given us this command: Whoever loves God must also love his brother.***
>
> ***(I John 4:8-10,19-21)***

Again we can see that *"no tweaking up"* that which is CARNAL, *no keeping* of any part of the *law* , *no good intentions*, no matter how noble, or lofty, will ever cause this change in flow-direction. It will only come by the *receiving of Christ* within, the RENEWING of the HOLY SPIRIT; the plugging in again of the lifeline that will make us the spiritually new man or woman. Only the *new birth*, a reconnection to God's spiritual lifeline, will again brighten up our darkened screen. This will then allow us to take proper actions which are pleasing to God.

The new birth requires a complete *dying* of *self* and *self efforts*, the acknowledging of our lost condition and the *embracing* of the grace and LOVE OF GOD. It is not something we grow into-but it is an instantaneous action that takes place by the determined will of the mind.

THIS IS SALVATION. This is the ONLY ROAD TO ETERNAL LIFE - there is no other! Search the world over, there will be found no other way! All others are not of God's doing and thus are self efforts or self works.

> ***For it is by grace you have been saved, through faith - and this not from yourselves, it is the gift of God - not by works, so that no one can boast. For we are God's workmanship, created in Christ Jesus to do good works, which God prepared in advance for us to do. (Ephesians 2:8-10)***

All people have been *imprisoned*, some physically, but *all spiritually*. Only the Lord has the keys to open the door and set us free from this *imprisonment*. He holds the keys to LIFE and DEATH. He is the Creator and the maker of all things. He is the giver of the laws (or rules) that define moral conduct, the judge of such conduct and the parole authority all in one.

Positive Steps To Right Decisions

SATAN'S LIE

Why do we insist on accepting Satan's lie that we shall not surely die when a quarter of a million people die each day the world goes round? The results of sin are evident on every hand in the grand procession of tears, sorrow, despair and death on every side. Why try and operate outside God's established system when there is no other authority, no other hope, or basis for life or eternal life given to man than that offered by God through Jesus Christ.

> ***Be imitators of God, therefore, as dearly loved children and live a life of love, just as Christ loved us and gave himself up for us as a fragrant offering and sacrifice to God. But among you there must not be even a hint of sexual immorality, or of any kind of impurity, or of greed, because these are improper for God's holy people. Nor should there be obscenity, foolish talk or coarse joking, which are out of place, but rather thanksgiving. For of this you can be sure: No immoral, impure or greedy person — such a man is an idolater — has any inheritance in the kingdom of Christ and of God. Let no one deceive you with empty words, for because of such things God's wrath comes on those who are disobedient. Therefore do not be partners with them. (Ephesians 5:1-7)***

I'm not going to be naive enough to suggest to you that in accepting Christ as Savior your present problems are ALL going to disappear, that *all* your troubles will *vanish over night.* I am not suggesting that as Paul and Silas sang in prison in stocks and bonds, as recorded in Acts 16:26-31, that a great earthquake will come and the gates to the prison will swing open and an angel of the Lord will lead you outside to freedom. That would be nice if it would be true today. I'm sure there would be many disenchanted prisoners getting very interested in the Word of God, perhaps not necessarily for salvation, but for an immediate and quick release some dark night.

Of course we must remember Paul and Silas were disciples of Christ and were on a special mission for Him and had been put in prison because they were OBEYING CHRIST by *spreading* the good news of the gospel. They had done no wrong!

CHRIST IS SUFFICIENT

But I will guarantee you that upon acceptance of Christ you will find available to you, inner *strength* and *wisdom,* whether incarcerated or not, to cope with any problems you may have. A *peace* will come into your heart and life that will enable you to experience great contentment and to be able to bear up under any circumstance or situation in which you find yourself. All those thoughts that were brought out of the closet and laid bare in the beginning of this book can finally be put behind us. A new HOPE can be born within us as we meditate on the promises of the Word of God.

> ***Therefore, since we have been justified through faith, we have peace with God through our Lord Jesus Christ, through whom we have gained access by faith into this grace in which we now stand. And we rejoice in the hope of the glory of God. Not only so, but we also rejoice in our***

sufferings, because we know that suffering produces perseverance; perseverance, character; and character, hope. (Romans 5:1-4)

All the promises of better things to come, if not fully realized in this life, will be fulfilled in a future life. We may not be able to wipe out all the circumstances and webs we've woven for our present life or put all the broken egg shells back together that we've cracked, broken and scattered. We will be able to find that strength, patience, and understanding so necessary to *cope* with *present* life situations!

In addition we can look forward to more blessed *future hopes* promised by the God of all eternity.

But by faith we eagerly await through the spirit the righteousness for which we hope. (Galatians 5:5)

I have fought the good fight, I have finished the race, I have kept the faith. Now there is in store for me the crown of righteousness, which the Lord, the righteous Judge, will award to me on that day — and not only to me, but also to all who have longed for his appearing. (II Timothy 4:7-8)

We know that the whole creation has been groaning as in the pains of childbirth right up to the present time. Not only so, but we ourselves, who have the firstfruits of the Spirit, groan inwardly as we wait eagerly for our adoption as sons, the redemption of our bodies. For in this hope we were saved. But hope that is seen is no hope at all. Who hopes for what he already has? But if we hope for what we do not yet have, we wait for it patiently. (Romans 8:22-25)

How many around you are *anxious?* How many are rattling the bars of restraint? How many are striving with everything, everybody, every condition they find themselves in? How many are angry with everyone around them; loved ones, family, friends and associates? How many are truly disillusioned, disappointed, dejected and defeated with this present life? How many long for peace on earth? How many are missing true joy and fellowship with others and themselves because life has soured? How many really long for a peace in their hearts where regardless of circumstances or conditions, they can find contentment and satisfaction? How many? ALL OF US!

This may sound simplistic at first but there is only *one answer* to all *world problems.* World problems are just a collection and magnification of individual problems; yours and mine. I might also note that there is really only one big problem, "*sin*" which manifests itself in a variety of forms and results. Wars, hate, divorce, crime, disease, dishonesty and death are just a few offsprings of this monster.

WHAT IS THE ANSWER? The only answer to them all is JESUS CHRIST - God's Son. You're probably thinking "it can't be that simple. It can't be that unique. It can't be that dynamic or dramatic." How do you know until you try? Haven't you and others you know tried about every other recipe in the cook book but this one? Many millions, of all ages and all walks of life testify that IT'S TRUE, praise God, IT'S TRUE; once they've sampled and tasted the results.

Jesus said "my yoke is easy, my burden is light. If you are heavy laden, try me." Won't you try Jesus? Haven't you and past generations tried about everything else imaginable? Jesus is *God's response* to our *waywardness,* our *rebellion,* our SINS.

> ***"Come to me, all you who are weary and burdened, and I will give you rest. Take my yoke upon you and learn from me, for I am gentle and humble in heart, and you will find rest for your souls. For my yoke is easy and my burden is light." (Matthew 11:28-30)***

In Christ is found all the needed answers. You question, How could He be so all important? Because He spoke the universe into existence - He *created us* from the dust of the earth and He and He alone *can restore* our soul.

Come home! Come back to God! Move off your little personal stage with Satan as director. The act is about over. The lights are soon going to be turned out! The *curtain* is about to FALL! The judgment is about to begin! Then it will be too late for you to respond. Remember "It is appointed unto men once to die and after this the judgment."

POSITIVE STEPS

We read in Romans 10:9 these words, "If thou shalt confess with thy mouth the Lord Jesus Christ, and shalt *believe* in thine heart that God has raised Him from the dead, thou shalt be saved." Do you BELIEVE? By what other authority would you dare add or subtract any other conditions to God's statement?

We also note from the Holy Scriptures this admonition from Christ: *"repent* and be *baptized."*

Let's take a closer look at some of these words that God has used in these passages taken from His Holy Word - such words as: (1) *believe,* (2) *repent,* (3) *confess* and (4) *baptize.*

We are not going to spend much time here in review, but in case you are not a Christian already, these are extremely IMPORTANT words. Go to a dictionary and to the Bible and look up these words, and read for yourself what God says. These are simple and easily identified words, but are deep in meaning and content.

What does *believe* mean? The dictionary definition of belief is "to have faith in, to hold as true." To honestly believe anything, we must accept it fully in our heart as truth. We must believe to such an extent that all of our *future* ACTIONS express our belief. Our belief comes from faith in God's Word. The Scriptures say "faith cometh by hearing and hearing by the word of God." Thus, we must *hear* or *read* the Word of God before we can believe the things of God. But just to believe with head knowledge, or to merely assent by nodding our head that something is true, is not enough. Even the devils, the Scriptures note, believe in God and tremble but are still lost. WHY? Because they will *not obey* God's Word and accept Christ's Lordship! Heart belief implies CONFIRMING ACTION; heart belief *causes a change,* a different direction to life. Positive *steps toward God* and in God's way are *evidence* of heart belief.

> ***He then brought them out and asked, "Sirs, what must I do to be saved?"***
> ***They replied, "Believe in the Lord Jesus, and you will be saved — you and your household." (Acts 16:30-31)***

What does it mean to *repent?* Repent, among other things, means to turn about - to turn back TO GOD from your former way of life. It means to give up and to REJECT THAT SINFUL WALK that previously has been motivated by self. It means to accept God's way and His instruction.

I tell you, no! But unless you repent, you too will all perish. (Luke 13:3)

What does it mean to *confess?* Confess means to acknowledge with our lips that which has been done or that which we know to be true. In coming to God we must first acknowledge and confess to Him that we have "sinned and come short of His glory." Secondly, we must confess or proclaim His name to others. We must acknowledge that Jesus Christ is the Son of God as we accept Him as our Lord and Savior. Christ is the one, the only one, with the power to forgive sins. By confessing Christ, our past sins can be justified before a just and Holy God, and wiped off the record book.

That if you confess with your mouth, "Jesus is Lord," and believe in your heart that God raised him from the dead, you will be saved. For it is with your heart that you believe and are justified, and it is with your mouth that you confess and are saved. (Romans 10:9-10)

I like that! I need that! I appreciate that easily understood, straight forward promise from God! Why is Baptism important? Regarding baptism, this is the first act of obedience God asks of us, after we have believed, repented and made a confession of faith. Baptism is an outward public confession of the inward change. A change that says we really believe, accept, and are willing to obey the Word of God. Even Jesus obeyed this command and was praised by God, the Father. When Jesus was being baptised by John, as He arose from the water of the Jordan River, the Holy Spirit was seen descending on Him in the form of a dove, and God's voice from Heaven was heard saying, "This is my beloved Son in whom I am well pleased. HEAR YE HIM." If we are not willing to follow this expressed command of God as our first act of obedience, how can any future acts we perform be pleasing to God?

> ***He said to them, "Go into all the world and preach the good news to all creation. Whoever believes and is baptized will be saved, but whoever does not believe will be condemned. (Mark 16:15, 16)***

When we take these *right* steps, God's spirit, the HOLY SPIRIT, comes to dwell with us. It *is* HE that will begin to shape and control our lives, bringing into remembrance the things of God.

> ***But I tell you the truth: It is for your good that I am going away. Unless I go away, the Counselor will not come to you; but if I go, I will send him to you. When he comes, he will convict the world of guilt in regard to sin and righteousness and judgment:***
>
> ***But when he, the Spirit of truth, comes, he will guide you into all truth. He will not speak on his own; he will speak only what he hears, and he will tell you what is yet to come. He will bring glory to me by taking from what is mine and making it known to you. (John 16:7-8, 13, 14)***

Maybe as Christians we've made the good confession but have strayed from the Word. Our conversation and communing with God is NOT what it used to be or should be! Our *self-will* is *still evident* on our heart's throne, replacing God's Will at almost every opportunity. If this be the case in your life, then return to His Holy Word and in PRAYER, ask for forgiveness and guidance. For only in so doing will we be able to renew our fellowship and walk in obedience to His Word and be pleasing in His sight.

By the guidance of the Holy Spirit, the love of Christ will begin to reflect through us to others and we will finally begin to bear the fruit of true Christians. We can never change or *shape up* by self effort, by bargaining or trade-offs or by logic or reasoning on our own. Only by the power of the resurrected Christ, living in us and through us, can the change be made. It is only as we come back in complete surrender of ourselves, in complete confession of the helplessness of our own abilities, that God can work through us or use us. We must come JUST AS WE ARE, in our weakness, in our sins, and bring *all* to Christ for cleansing! "If we confess our sins, He is faithful and just to forgive us our sins, and to cleanse us from ALL UNRIGHTEOUSNESS." (Ref. 1 John 1:9)

We can come to God, whether on beds of pain and sorrow, in times of imprisonment, in tears or joy, or when we are in the best of health and spirit. But, we must realize that in ourselves we have NO worthiness, merit, or capability for change. It is *only* under these humbling circumstances that God can accept or help us. God says, "Now is the accepted time." Yes, the time for self-will and ego to be trampled into the dust and buried. Many times God can only get through to us in moments such as these periods in our life when we are experiencing many trials and great suffering. He often uses our very illness, infirmities and hopelessness as another opportunity to *once again* speak to us since the pace of normal living is dimmed into the background.

Previously we couldn't understand, we didn't hear, *we didn't have the time* to listen to the voice of God speaking patiently and quietly to us in our inner being. But now, perhaps we can begin to comprehend that we, as created beings, do not really have control over the things of the world, over our health, over our next heartbeat or breath, over this life, or over the things of the next life, except, maybe, to dissipate or shorten this physical life we now possess. When we come to this elementary realization, perhaps for the first time in our life, we have now taken the first in a series of *right steps* back to God. This first step of awareness must be taken so God can begin to communicate in LOVE to you and to me.

COME

What are the steps involved in coming to God?

First come to God in the quietness of your very being and your inner thoughts and acknowledge Him for who He is. Close your eyes and acknowledge your sinful and wayward condition before Him, and ask Christ to forgive you of all your sins. ASK Jesus Christ to come into your heart for a cleansing and refreshing and *to permanently live* and *abide with you*. He is willing to be your constant companion through the remaining part of this life and throughout all the ages to come. If we take an honest survey of our lives we will undoubtedly find that we are spiritually bankrupt and surprisingly, totally dependent on God for all our physical needs and blessings. Thus for spiritual renewal, forgiveness of sins, and physical healing WE NEED JESUS. He promised, 'Behold, I stand at the door and knock: If any man hear my voice and open the door, I will come in.' (Ref. Revelation 3:20)

He's knocking! Open the door and invite Him in!

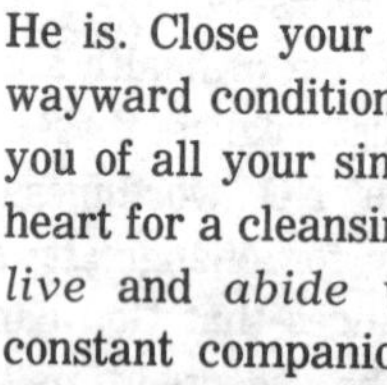

If we come to God in this manner; in confession, with praise and acknowledgement, abiding in the promises of His Word, He says that we may ask what we will, and it will be done unto us.

Abiding in His Word is one of the conditions to answered prayer. As non-Christians we can expect none of our prayers to be answered except this one, "God be merciful to me, a sinner, and save me in Jesus name." But this one goes direct to the throne of God!

If you make or have already made this great decision of life to accept Jesus Christ as your Lord and Savior, you can find peace in the remaining days, weeks and years of your life. As you commune with God in prayer and seek His Word, you can receive a new personality, have a new life and obtain new hope. A new SPIRITUAL BIRTH will truly be yours as you surrender self and return to God.

The imprisonments, trials, the illnesses, the troubles, the pain, and the tribulations of our day may remain for awhile but each of these can be put in their proper perspective, for God *can* and will provide the grace and love, the peace and joy, the strength and wisdom sufficient for our every need - even in *death*.

Today He can become your guide as you allow Him his rightful place in your life. My prayer is that through this communication you may be introduced to the One who made you and gave you *this life*, to the One who can save you and give you ETERNAL LIFE. Accept Him and His gift right now! Ask God for the faith to believe His promises and the *wisdom to discern* His Word.

I invite you to come out of the encircling web of your sins,to loose yourself from the restraining and entangling ways of the world that Satan has so cleverly woven and to *step out* as a new creation into the glorious freedom and sunshine of God's love. The transformation will be as dramatic as a lowly worm crawling from under the darkness of a bushy plant to be miraculously changed to a glorious beautiful butterfly, equipped with silky wings to fly among the beautiful flowers, under the blue skies and brilliant sunshine of God's new day.

Let God take charge of your ruined life and redeem it and give you a new spiritual birth so He can eventually resurrect you,as He makes you fit for all eternity.

Come *today* even to the Master's house. As you hear the knock on your heart's door, open it in prayer, confessing your true condition, your needs, your desires, and INVITE JESUS to come in and abide - to be your Lord; your Savior; your guide. If you are sincere in your repentence and requests, the TRANSFORMATION WILL BE ACCOMPLISHED *immediately* by Christ Himself!

All this will resound to the glory of God the Father, Creator of the universe and all that is therein. But more importantly it will *redeem you*, as an individual, from a life headed for death row - to LIFE ETERNAL. It will make you a recipient of God's Spirit and His great love. You will become a literal heir of the universe with Jesus Christ, who alone is your Creator, who alone can redeem you, who alone can be your true Lord and Savior. You *can* become a SON OF GOD! You *can* experience the NEW BIRTH and be a recipient of God's great gift of ETERNAL LIFE!

ASK TODAY . . . *for there is no other way . . .*

BUT JESUS!

Praise the Lord.

Praise the Lord, O my soul.
I will praise the Lord all my life;
I will sing praise to my God as long as I live.

Do not put your trust in princes,
in mortal men, who cannot save.
When their spirit departs, they return to the ground;
on that very day their plans come to nothing.

Blessed is he whose help is the God of Jacob,
whose hope is in the Lord his God,
the Maker of heaven and earth,
the sea, and everything in them —
the Lord, who remains faithful forever.
He upholds the cause of the oppressed
and gives food to the hungry.
The Lord sets prisoners free,
the Lord gives sight to the blind,
the Lord lifts up those who are bowed down,
the Lord loves the righteous.
The Lord watches over the alien
and sustains the fatherless and the widow,
but he frustrates the ways of the wicked.

The Lord reigns forever,
your God, O Zion, for all generations.

Praise the Lord.

Psalm 146

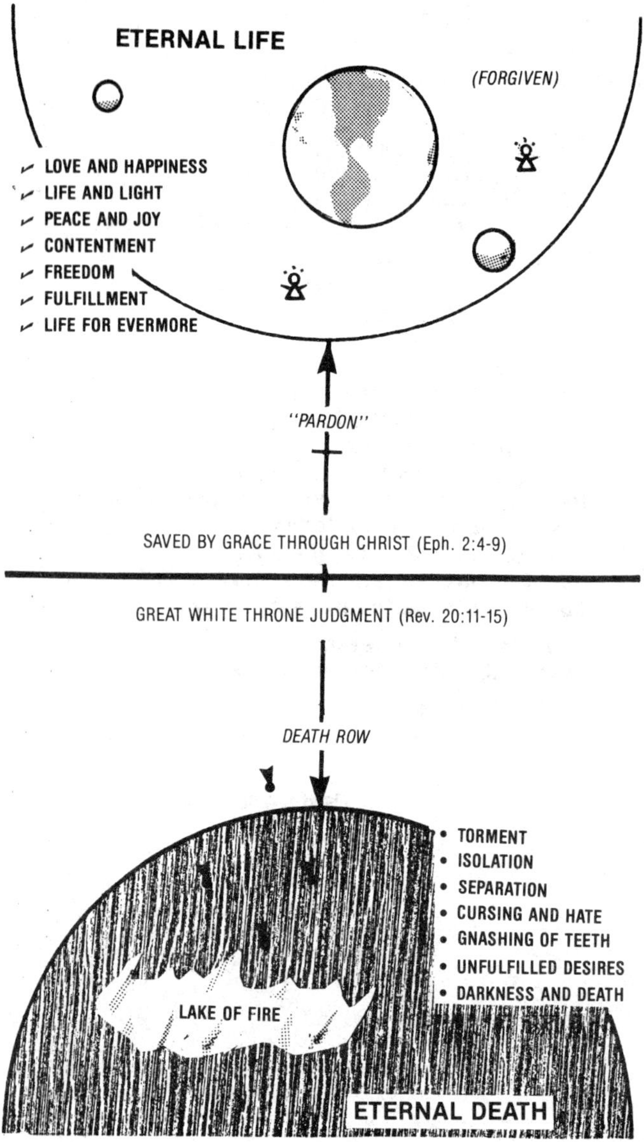

ETERNAL LIFE
(FORGIVEN)
LOVE AND HAPPINESS
LIFE AND LIGHT
PEACE AND JOY
CONTENTMENT
FREEDOM
FULFILLMENT
LIFE FOR EVERMORE
"PARDON"
SAVED BY GRACE THROUGH CHRIST (Eph. 2:4-9)
GREAT WHITE THRONE JUDGMENT (Rev. 20:11-15)
DEATH ROW
TORMENT
ISOLATION
SEPARATION
CURSING AND HATE
GNASHING OF TEETH
UNFULFILLED DESIRES
DARKNESS AND DEATH
LAKE OF FIRE
ETERNAL DEATH

RECOMMITMENT TIME

MY DECISION: I acknowledge that I have **not** been obeying and following the Lord in a manner worthy of the name "Christian" which I previously accepted. I have grieved the Holy Spirit and have ignored the final sacrifice that Christ made for me on Calvary's cross.

I again acknowledge and repent of my worldliness, my sins and self-indulgence which keeps me from doing those things which are pleasing to you, O Lord. Henceforth I will rely upon You by **faith** for all my present and future needs. I will prayerfully study the Scriptures to find Your daily will for my life, and will be faithful in presenting my praise and petitions to You, who created and redeemed me.

Date ______________ Signature ____________________________

DECISION TIME

MY DECISION: Acknowledging that I am a sinner, and believing that Jesus Christ the Son of God was crucified for me, arose again from the dead and is now sitting at the right hand of God the Father as High Priest, I now, by faith, receive Him into my heart and life as my personal Savior. I will repent of my sins and at the first opportunity, I will confess Him before others and will be baptized. I will faithfully study the Bible to find God's will for my life.

Date ______________ *Signature* ____________________________

NEW TESTAMENT SCRIPTURES

The following compilation of references grouped by major subjects has been complied by Watson Goodman, World Missionary Press, New Paris, IN 46553.

Used by permission.

PRAYER, THE WAY TO UNDEFEATABLE VICTORY

Requests for Prayer
Acts 8:24
Romans 15:30
Ephesians 6:19
I Thessalonians 5:25
II Thessalonians 3:1
Hebrews 13:18

Unwise Request to God
Matthew 20:21-23

The Old Testament teaches that disobedience, secret sin, indifference, neglect of mercy, despising the law, blood-guiltiness, iniquity, stubbornness are causes of failure in prayer.
Matthew 5:23, 24
Matthew 6:14, 15
Romans 8:26
James 1:5-8; 4:3

Private Prayer
Matthew 6:6
Acts 10:9
Acts 10:30

United Prayer
Matthew 18:19
Luke 1:10
Acts 1:14; 4:24
Acts 12:12
Acts 21:5

Always Have a Right Spirit
Psalm 51:10: Create in me a clean heart, O God; and renew a right spirit within me.

Victorious Spiritual Warfare
Acts 4:13, 29-31
Acts 9:29; 19:8
Romans 1:16
I Corinthians 10:12, 13
I Corinthians 16:13
II Corinthians 10:4, 5
Ephesians 6:11-17
I Thessalonians 5:8, 9, 23
I Timothy 6:12
II Timothy 2:4
Hebrews 12:1, 2
James 4:7, 8
I Peter 5:8-10

Christ's True Followers Are Overcomers
John 16:33
Romans 12:21
I John 4:4
I John 5:4, 5
Revelation 2:7, 10, 17
Revelation 2:26-28
Revelation 3:5, 12, 21
Revelation 15:2, 3
Revelation 20:4, 6
Revelation 21:7, 8

PRAYER, THE WAY TO UNDEFEATABLE VICTORY

Pray to the Father, in Jesus' Name, in the Holy Spirit
John 14:13; 16:23
Jude 20

"Prayer Is Talking with God."

The Basis of Prayer
Romans 8:15
Romans 10:13
Hebrews 10:19-22

Admonitions To Pray
Matthew 7:7, 8
Matthew 26:41
Luke 18:1
John 16:24
Ephesians 6:18
I Thessalonians 5:17
James 5:13

The Holy Spirit Aids in Prayer
Romans 8:26, 27

Ask in Accord with God's Will
II Corinthians 12:8, 9
James 4:3
I John 5:14, 15

Be Specific When You Pray
Matthew 6:7; 23:14
Luke 18:13; 23:34
Luke 23:42
Acts 7:60

What To Pray About
Matthew 14:19
Romans 10:1, 13
James 1:5
Matthew 6:9-13
James 5:14-16
I Timothy 2:2
Matthew 5:44; 6:10
I John 1:9
Philippians 4:6

Conditions of Successful Prayer

II Chronicles 7:14: If my people, which are called by my name, shall humble themselves, and pray, and seek my face, and turn from their wicked ways; then will I hear from heaven, and will forgive their sin, and will heal their land.

Jeremiah 29:13: And ye shall seek me, and find me, when ye shall search for me with all your heart.

Matthew 21:21, 22
Mark 11:24
Luke 11:5-8
I John 3:22

Praise God in Prayer
Hebrews 13:15

Prayers of Saints Are Precious
Revelation 5:8; 8:3, 4

Promises To Answer Prayer
Luke 11:9
John 15:7

Persist in Prayer
Luke 11:5-13; 18:1-8

Examples of Christ Praying
Mark 1:35; 6:46, 47
Luke 5:15, 16; 6:12
Matthew 11:25, 26
Luke 3:21
Luke 9:18; 22:41, 42
John 11:41; 17:1

Christ Gave a Model Prayer
Matthew 6:9-13
Luke 11:2-4

VICTORIOUS LIVING IN CHRIST JESUS

Faith To Overcome the World
I John 5:4
Romans 5:1
Ephesians 6:16
I Thessalonians 5:8
I Timothy 6:12
Hebrews 10:19-25
Hebrews 11:6
James 1:5, 6

What Jesus Taught About Faith
Matthew 9:22
Mark 9:23
Luke 7:3-9, 50
Luke 8:48-50
Luke 18:8
John 6:28, 29
John 11:25, 26

Grow to Maturity in Christ
I Corinthians 3:1, 2
Ephesians 4:13-16
I Timothy 4:12-16
Hebrews 5:11-14

Accept Your Stewardship
Matthew 12:36; 18:23
Matthew 25:14-30
Luke 12:48
Romans 14:12
I Corinthians 4:2
I Corinthians 6:20
I Thessalonians 2:4
I Timothy 1:11
I Peter 4:10

Spiritual Abundance in Christ
John 1:16
John 15:11
II Corinthians 4:16, 17
II Corinthians 9:8
Ephesians 3:16-20
Philippians 4:19
Colossians 2:19; 3:10
I Timothy 1:14

Abound in Victory in Christ
II Corinthians 2:14
II Corinthians 10:4
Romans 8:37
Philippians 1:9, 10

Peace, Rest in a Troubled World
Matthew 11:28, 29
Luke 1:78, 79
Luke 2:13, 14
John 14:27; 16:33
Acts 10:36
Romans 5:1; 8:6
Romans 14:17
Galatians 5:22, 23
Ephesians 2:14
Philippians 4:7
Colossians 1:20
Hebrews 4:3

Holiness, Our Way of Life
Luke 1:74, 75
Romans 6:19, 22
II Corinthians 7:1
Ephesians 1:4; 4:24
I Thessalonians 3:13
I Thessalonians 4:7
I Timothy 2:15
Titus 2:3
Hebrews 12:10, 14
I Peter 1:15
II Peter 3:11

Be Filled with the Spirit
Luke 11:13
Acts 1:8; 2:1-6
Acts 4:31; 7:55
Acts 11:24; 13:52
Romans 8:9

CHRIST SHARES WITH THE TRUE BELIEVERS

His Nature
John 14:20
Philippians 3:21
Hebrews 3:14
II Peter 1:4

His Character
Luke 1:74, 75
Romans 6:4; 8:29
Galatians 5:22-24
Ephesians 4:13, 24
I Peter 1:16; 2:9
II Peter 1:3, 5-10

His Victory
I Corinthians 15:20-23
I Corinthians 15:57
I John 5:4, 5
Revelation 2:26; 3:21
Revelation 15:2; 17:14

His Glory
John 17:22-24
II Peter 1:3
Colossians 3:4

His Relationships
John 20:17
Ephesians 3:17, 19
Colossians 1:27
Hebrews 2:11
I John 3:24
Revelation 3:20

His Service
Mark 10:43-45
John 14:12; 21:16
Galatians 6:2, 10
I Peter 4:11

His Suffering
II Corinthians 1:5
Philippians 3:10
I Peter 4:1

His Name
Matthew 18:20
John 14:13
John 17:11, 12; 20:31
Acts 3:6, 16; 16:18
Ephesians 5:20

His Peace
John 14:27; 16:33
Romans 1:7
Galatians 5:22
Ephesians 2:14
Colossians 3:15
II Thessalonians 3:16

His Joy
Luke 15:4-6
John 15:11; 16:24; 17:13
Romans 14:17

His Possessions
Romans 8:17
I Corinthians 3:21-23
Hebrews 1:14; 6:17
James 2:5

His Experiences
Matthew 10:24, 25
Luke 6:40
John 15:18-21
John 17:23, 26
Galatians 2:20

His Worldwide Soul-Winning
Matthew 28:18-20
Mark 16:14-18
Luke 24:44-49
John 20:21
Acts 1:8

His Results of Soul-Winning
Revelation 5:9, 10
Revelation 7:9, 15-17

His Eternal Throne
Luke 22:28-30
Revelation 3:21; 5:10

THE BELIEVER'S POSITION AND BENEFITS

Christ in the Redeemed
John 17:23
Romans 8:9
I Corinthians 3:16
Galatians 2:20
Ephesians 3:17, 19
Colossians 1:27
I John 3:24
Revelation 3:20

The Redeemed in Christ
John 14:20; 15:5, 7
John 16:33
I Corinthians 1:30
II Corinthians 1:21
II Corinthians 5:17
Galatians 6:15
Philippians 3:9

The Redeemed in Christ's Body
Romans 12:5
I Corinthians 12:27
Ephesians 1:22, 23; 4:12
Colossians 1:24

Christ Exalted
Mark 16:19
Luke 22:69
John 5:23
Acts 2:36; 5:31
Ephesians 1:20-22
Philippians 2:9-11
Hebrews 1:9
I Peter 3:22
Revelation 5:12, 13

Saints Exalted with Christ
Luke 19:17; 22:28, 29
Romans 5:17
I Corinthians 6:2
II Timothy 2:12
Revelation 1:5, 6; 3:21
Revelation 20:4

Sitting in Heavenly Places
Ephesians 1:17-21
Ephesians 2:4-9
Revelation 1:6; 3:21
Revelation 20:6
Revelation 22:3-5

Walking with Christ
Ephesians 4:1, 2, 17-32
Ephesians 5:2, 8-17
Philippians 1:6

Standing with Christ in Warfare
Romans 8:37
Ephesians 6:10-18

Believers Use Name of Christ
Mark 16:17, 18
Luke 10:17-20
John 14:13, 14
John 15:16
John 16:23-27
Acts 4:7-12
Acts 16:18
Philippians 2:9-11
Revelation 19:16

Sons of God
Matthew 5:9
Luke 20:36
John 1:12
Romans 8:14-21
II Corinthians 6:17, 18
Galatians 4:5-7
Philippians 2:14, 15
I John 3:1, 10

Joint Heirs with Christ
Romans 8:17
Galatians 3:29
Galatians 4:7
Titus 3:7
Hebrews 1:14
Hebrews 6:17

ABOUT THE AUTHOR

CONNELLY GRAHAM, DESIGN ENGINEER, EXAMINING A MODEL OF THE "TITAN INTERCONTINENTAL BALLISTIC MISSILE."

Connelly Graham, a registered professional engineer, has worked on America's top air-power secrets for 23 years. He established the configuration design of the first 5000 mile missile in 1946 and in a five year period assigned eight classified patents to major corporations. Many jet aircraft and missiles flying today reflect his earlier creative ability. In 1964 he resigned all his engineering positions and was ordained into the ministry. Preaching in hundreds of churches in the United States and around the world, he is founder and director, serving without pay, of an inter-denominational mission organization, "Christians in Action" – now headquarterd in Indiana.

Under his guidance, special audio visual programs, one-hour puppet programs and multi-media presentations featuring a 70 to 80 percent direct quote of the scriptures, have been developed for foreign mission use and for showing in churches.

Untold thousands have read his many articles and booklets such as "The Lost World," "How to Personal Witness," "Are You Having Troubles," "Don't Go Yet," "A Letter to My Sister," and "So You're in the Hospital." An illustrated booklet of scriptures, "The Bible Speaks," has been translated into four different languages.

The latest literature to be developed and distributed throughout English and Spanish speaking nations is a series of five different "Life Guide" charts, outlining the whole of the Bible in chart form from Genesis to Revelation. Each item on the chart is indexed to pertinent scriptural verses. Some charts include as many as 1500 such references, permitting use as a visual concordance or as a guide for home Bible study programs.

Mr. Graham is burdened and concerned for the millions who do not yet know the saving power of Jesus Christ. He has been equally saddened by the apathy and spiritual unconcern shown by many professing Christians.. The tremendous response from inmates in penitentiaries where Christians in Action literature has been distributed, coupled with the above concerns, has prompted the writing of this unique poignant book, **ESCAPE FROM IMPRISONMENT,** which covers many facets of the Christian walk.